COURTYARD
LIVING

Charmaine Chan

COURTYARD LIVING

Contemporary Houses
of the Asia-Pacific

WITH 275 ILLUSTRATIONS

CONTENTS

INTRODUCTION

Do not take dictionary definitions at face value. I learnt that lesson a few years ago when I turned to my *Concise Oxford English Dictionary* to reply to Thames & Hudson. I remember being surprised by their keen but guarded response to my initial pitch for a book on twenty-first-century courtyard houses, which, they said, was potentially a very large subject, with many dimensions. Perhaps I needed to define my intended audience and specify the kinds of dwellings I had in mind.

Envisaging my readers was easy: design-literate, style-conscious (would-be) home owners. Describing courtyard houses – and the term 'courtyard' itself – was decidedly more difficult, even though explanations of both abound.

I particularly liked one definition of the courtyard as simply a 'social device' that 'identifies a communal place'.[1] Privacy was the priority in many descriptions, and important too were the courtyard's exterior nature and function as a basic organizing element in architectural layouts. Additionally, the area was often associated with activity, and courtyard houses were described as having L, U, H or O shapes. However, the examples I include in this book go beyond these descriptions and show how courtyards can be conceptual and amorphous as well as visual and functional.

Instead of setting the parameters, I had architects tell me what they understood courtyards to be. But to control the scope of this book I confined my survey to a selection of the latest contemporary courtyard houses in the Asia-Pacific region, meaning, in the main, homes in warm climes and on my turf. I also examined designs that put the courtyard at the heart of the house, or gave it immediate physical or visual connections to main living areas, making it an outdoor room open to the sky.

But wasn't this obvious, I wondered, randomly picturing a couple of old favourites. One is the architectural benchmark Schindler House – built in 1922, in West Hollywood, California – partly because it allowed its creator, Rudolph Schindler, and his wife, Pauline, to fulfil their 'revisionist' lifestyle: dining outdoors, sleeping beneath the stars and sharing their home with others. In the 1930s, when the good times came to an end for the couple, they lived separately – but together – in their three-courtyard modernist house.

I also conjured up Alison and Peter Smithson's 1956 one-bedroom, windowless townhouse, featuring an internal garden. Their theoretical design, entered in a 'House of the Future' competition, was the star of the London *Daily Mail* Ideal Home Exhibition that year.

From my side of the world, nothing so modern immediately emerged. I thought of the quadrangle houses detailed in Ronald Knapp's many books about China's architectural heritage and recalled the family compound in Zhang Yimou's evocative *Raise the Red Lantern*. That 1991 film, based on a novel by Su Tong, captured the cloistered world of long-suffering mistresses, each of whom inhabited a small courtyard dwelling that would be lit seductively on those nights she found favour with her master.

The courtyards above take on different roles as well as shapes and sizes, but all are open to the heavens while being integral to the buildings that surround them. Key is the indoor–outdoor relationship, an attribute,

Opposite: Louvres at 3 Houses, Vietnam (see page 210), are an integral part of the design, allowing light into the buildings while also providing shade in the central courtyard.

according to Australian academic Robert Nelson, underscored by fusing together 'court' (of law, for instance, which almost always convenes under a roof) and 'yard' (front or back).

Nelson also argues, in a fascinating paper probing the courtyard's lexical weakness, for the difficulty of definition. Even property agents can be unsure of its meaning, he observes, which is why some choose 'courtyard' instead of 'garden' to avoid overstatement when referring to a modest outdoor space. The courtyard, he concludes, has 'an impeccable derivation but an insecure definition'.[2]

Despite – or perhaps because of – that, all the architects featured in this book have created confident expressions of courtyards. Their houses add different dimensions to the OED's somewhat rigid appraisal of the word, which means, the lexicographer decided (probably with eyes shut tight), 'an open area enclosed by walls or buildings, especially in a castle or large house'.

Nowhere does the dictionary mention the courtyard's centrality, which is just as well, because I felt freer to seek out new domestic examples of a design typology that has been around for millennia, with courtyards not necessarily at their core. An interesting example is the subterranean Riparian House, on the outskirts of Mumbai, which relies on a 6 x 4-metre (20 x 13-ft) void at the back for comfort (see pages 180–189).

And calling a house 'large', of course, is subjective. While some homes in my selection are sizeable (500 square metres/5,380 sq ft or more), most are about the size of an average Australian home (235.8 square metres/2,538 sq ft, in 2020). Some even verged on small, among them the 150-square-metre (1,610-sq-ft) 3 Houses, wedged into an awkward plot in Ho Chi Minh City, Vietnam (see pages 210–217).

Indeed, I left a few houses out of this book simply because they and their courtyards felt too big. Had I known I would feel that way about what is usually a real-estate advantage, I probably would not have insisted on seeing them. Their outdoor spaces, bounded by buildings, no less, felt like gardens or lawns because they lacked a sense of intimacy.

These areas had perhaps lost their 'courtyardness' because their designers had ignored calculations used by their forebears to determine the appropriate proportions (which vary from culture to culture). Or maybe they hadn't considered these circumscribed areas outdoor rooms, which usually benefit from a human scale.

The working definition of courtyard was confining in other ways too. Randy Chan, of Singapore-based Zarch Collaboratives, declares that light, not walls, can be used to define a courtyard. His opinion becomes immediately clear when you enter Ficus House and see in the middle of the ground floor a *Ficus benjamina* that is an axis mundi connecting Heaven and Earth (see pages 74–81). Shafts of light delineate the courtyard containing the tree.

In Sri Lanka, Palinda Kannangara describes the courtyards at Artists' Studio as 'breathing spaces' (see pages 238–245), an idea that Vietnamese architect Toan Nghiem picks up and runs with in Saigon House, whose courtyard is not so much the hemmed-in open area, he insists, but the movement of air through the building (see pages 202–209).

A courtyard is made up of good sensations, he seems to say.

I remembered Nghiem during my correspondence with exuberant Sri Lankan architect and scholar C. Anjalendran. An assistant to Geoffrey Bawa early in their respective careers, Anjalendran suggested I start my exploration of Sri Lankan courtyard houses with the Ena de Silva House, designed by Bawa and built in Colombo in the early 1960s. 'That house is the precursor to all contemporary courtyard houses in Asia,' he said, adding what is probably my favourite statement among many by architects I spoke to for this book: 'Each culture [in Sri Lanka] – the Sinhalese, Tamils, Muslims, Dutch – used courtyards differently,' he wrote in an email. 'But clearly the traditional courtyard was a utilitarian space, while the present one is based on PLEASURE!!!'

That is true for each of the twenty-five houses in this book, all completed in the 2010s, and 'new' also because many will set aesthetic trends in discretion: several of the houses in this collection show off blank façades; not a few boast exposed concrete and brickwork; and most have only one or two storeys above ground.

Among my favourites – for its appealing anonymity from the street and visual gratification the moment you step inside – is Jakarta's AW House, by Andra Matin (see pages 16–25). A stooped moringa tree in the courtyard is the prize exhibit in a collection of extraordinary artwork. It is the focus of the house because it lends such joy.

Although courtyards feature prominently in many of Matin's domestic dwellings, the Indonesian architect avoids calling them that. To him they are simply positive spaces that allow sightlines through a house configured solid, void, solid.

Such an explanation for his 'accidental' courtyards is, however, inadequate, as we both discovered. Although such a setup similarly describes his own residence, I hesitated to include it after Matin wrote to say that, on reflection, his was not a courtyard house after all. A couple of years after my first tour of his home, I revisited the central outdoor area between his and his wife's discrete two-storey private suite and the house accommodating their children and the living area. He was right. The patch of grass I had in mind did not feel private and, surely, privacy is a major reason for having a courtyard – or two.

I had arrived at this conclusion via a decades-long trans-Pacific route, sidetracked by an architecture project: my own courtyard house in Sydney, Australia. However, not until construction started on 2 + 2 House (see pages 108–117) did I realize how much I craved the freedom that comes with privacy. Living cheek by jowl for years in Hong Kong was probably to blame. But for me, refuge beat prospect any day, though having both is an irresistible challenge.

For inspiration I looked for, but could not find, illustrated books on twenty-first-century courtyard houses – which was odd because shelter-magazine and newspaper articles seemed to suggest the typology was enjoying a revival. I discovered, at least in the cities I visited, that courtyard houses are still a niche choice for such factors as smaller plot size; cost (because of additional exterior surfaces);

setback rules in suburbs; and the natural tendency to want more, not less (in terms of gross floor area). That is why my book features no contemporary courtyard houses in Hong Kong, one of the world's most expensive property markets.

I did find plenty of academic research into the history of courtyard houses across the globe. This helped convince me that if the type of dwelling had survived since antiquity – in the Middle East, China, North Africa – there must be good reasons for puncturing a building to capture outdoor space.

But what are the reasons for building courtyard houses today, and how do they differ from those of yore?

The answers vary. Like their predecessors, all the courtyard houses I visited use the device to provide natural sources of light and ventilation – an especially salient topic because of pandemic-heightened fears of contagion. After all, courtyards allow you to go out without "going out". Architects also insert interior gardens to meet that oft-heard desire to connect with nature. The ways in which their clients interact with the great outdoors, however, differ: some prefer it behind glass; others want it abstract, paved, stepped, watery or furnished.

Many courtyards were created for specific reasons: Cabildo Residence, in Manila, needed a noise barrier (see pages 46–51); House by the Lake, in Colombo, a meditative space (see pages 138–145); Marble House, in Bangkok, a 'private sky' (see pages 26–33); and Shadow House, near Mumbai, respite from the sun (see pages 168–179).

Then there was Bramston Residence in Brisbane, Australia, where I met busy parents relieved to be able to keep an eye on their children from almost anywhere in the house (see pages 146–155). Their central courtyard has a swimming pool.

Although every house I visited was special in some way, two homes moved me particularly because of my Chinese heritage. In Changhua, Tze-Chun Wei designed a contemporary version of a Chinese courtyard house on the roof of his father's factory to enable three generations of the family to live independently, yet as a unit, under the same roof (see pages 64–73). And in a Chinese enclave in Jakarta, AN House (see pages 34–45) raised its guard to address racial tensions that erupted into violence in 1998, resulting in the deaths of more than a thousand people. D-associates' inward-looking design is a reminder of other courtyard houses in history that have been built defensively.

I cannot remember visiting any courtyard houses during my childhood in Malaysia in the 1960s. I knew my father had spent his student years on the top floor of a Kuala Lumpur shophouse (then not something one boasted about), but the significance of this vernacular building type, characterized by its small courtyards (sometimes better described as air wells), did not interest me until later.

In my new home, Australia, had I been old enough in the 1970s to appreciate architecture I would undoubtedly have fallen in love with the modernist courtyard houses of Roy Grounds and Robin Boyd. As famous as their designs were, however, this type of dwelling never took hold in the sparsely populated Sydney suburbs of my youth, and no one I knew had an internal garden.

Then Japan happened to me. In the late 1980s and early 1990s, while working for a national newspaper in Tokyo, I went on excursions to the countryside and further afield, including to Kyoto, where I discovered *machiya*. I loved how those long, narrow townhouses, with delicate latticework fronts, made a fetish of small, perfectly formed inner gardens called *tsuboniwa* (a *tsubo* being an area equal to two tatami mats, or about 3½ square metres/35.5 sq ft).

Even after moving to Hong Kong on the eve of its handover to China in 1997, I followed the efforts of Japanophile Alex Kerr and others as they sought to preserve these *machiya* and their miniature landscapes. Japanese gardens, in their stylized forms, were captivating, but I admired them as one would museum exhibits that implore: look, don't touch.

It was not until a holiday in Penang, Malaysia, that I fully engaged with a courtyard that would shape my world. Shortly after its restoration in the 1990s, the Cheong Fatt Tze Mansion drew me in and sat me down in its central courtyard to deliver lessons about the wonder of symmetry, interior voids and that ineffable substance called 'chi'. For the only time in my life, I felt the energy of a building coursing through my body. Maybe it was the suggestion of feng shui perfection that gave me the shivers. Or perhaps I was feeling the delectable buzz of a world contained within walls – similar to the Earthly paradises that flowered centuries ago in Arabic courtyard houses.[3]

Fast-forward to the 2000s, when, in lasting admiration of Cheong Fatt Tze's mansion to mercantilism – known around the world as the Blue Mansion – I painted my village house in Hong Kong the same shade of indigo. Then came marriage and, after three decades working in Asia – the last third as the *South China Morning Post*'s design editor – the urge to build a house that would entice me back to Australia. In a brief I put together for Matt Elkan Architect, under the subtitle 'Would Like to Have' I wrote 'an internal courtyard garden'.

Mine was not so much a nostalgia for an imagined past as an attempt to find solutions to modern-day, first-world problems, among them the challenge of holding barbecues in blustery coastal winds. Also, priorities had changed since I first started thinking about courtyards. Wellness is now a growth industry and, as many home owners have told me, the courtyard house encourages a lifestyle with comfort at its core. Good ventilation and lighting help.

For me, the appeal of courtyard houses in the twenty-first century is enhanced by contemporary design that speaks of the past. More important than whether courtyards are completely or partially surrounded by rooms, or at the centre of a house or elsewhere, is the sense of enclosure they afford, as well as privacy, security and shelter.

I can think of another reason why they will continue to thrive. As one architect insisted wryly, a courtyard house gives him control of everything he sees: his architecture in the foreground, his landscape in the middle, and his architecture at the back. His bliss.

Perhaps 'paradise on Earth' should be tagged to any definition of the courtyard house. Lexicographers, are you listening?

Cheek-by-jowl development in [sub]urban areas forces architects to design introverted homes. These dwellings rely on courtyards for privacy and security – major attributes of the houses in this chapter. Marble House, which is surrounded by buildings, presents a stony face to the street. Its internal voids, however, perfectly frame sections of sky for exclusive enjoyment. Designed with protection in mind, the courtyards at AN House open the building from within, a boon in the event that shutters must come down outside. Apart from affording the kind of intimacy lacking in most front gardens and backyards, courtyards can also be showcases. Traffic-noise-defying Cabildo Residence uses its central garden as a beautiful backdrop for every room. Similarly, AW House has to tackle a busy road. Its focal point is an inner courtyard that commands movement around the house. The tree that stands in the middle is a breathtaking, private exhibit in a home full of impressive works.

AW HOUSE

Andra Matin

JAKARTA, INDONESIA, 2017

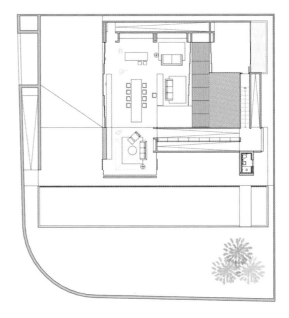

'A stair separates one storey from another; a ramp connects.' Modernism's maestro Le Corbusier made that remark in reference to the slopes he designed to link different levels at one of his most famous works: the Villa Savoye, in Poissy, France. In Jakarta's AW House, Indonesian architect Andra Matin builds on the concept by using a network of ramps to provide scenic routes between the ground floor and the rooftop garden two storeys above. These inclines provide gradual transitions between the levels and, combined with a courtyard, help Matin achieve his prime objective: 'I wanted every floor to feel like it's on the ground floor,' he says.

For aesthetic and practical reasons, Matin favours low-lying, 'skinny' houses that have a close relationship with the gardens around them. Ramps at AW House enhance that sense of oneness by encouraging fluid, unhurried movement through the different spaces and levels. At this 'woven' brick house, rooftop greenery, infinity ponds and generous planters outside bedrooms heighten the effect of every floor being grounded.

On the street level, the central courtyard and gardens on the periphery allow AW House to be enjoyed with its extensive Switchglass™ doors open, or closed with glass either clear or opaque. The four-bedroom, 812-square-metre (8,740-sq-ft) corner-plot residence, in the affluent enclave of Kebayoran Baru, is surrounded by buildings and faces a busy road.

Inverting the gaze made sense for those reasons, but in adhering to his preferred multilayered approach to residential design, Matin was able to create living areas with inward- *and* outward-facing vistas. 'I like the surprise you get from having layers,' he says, configuring rectangular objects close at hand (mobile phones, wallets) to explain his general design principle. 'I like to design houses that are void, solid, void, solid.'

The poolside veranda, open kitchen and living areas look out on to turf built up gradually so that, at its farthest reaches, it meets the top of a 2.8-metre-tall (9 ft) wall separating the property from the main road and a side street. The berm blocks views of vehicles, and, from within the compound,

Pages 12–13: Cut out of the middle of Marble House (see pages 26–33) is a courtyard that helps ventilate the house, with the help of several smaller voids.

Opposite: The moringa tree in the courtyard of AW House is a spectacle visible from many parts of the house, including the living areas, guest bedroom, ramp and stairs.

One aim was to have
every level feel as though
it were the ground floor.
Lemongrass in front of
two bedrooms above the
living areas accentuates
the effect.

gives the impression that you're anywhere but close to traffic.

Across the living areas the focus is on a lone moringa tree planted in the void at the heart of the house. Bent double, with a Medusa-like head of 'hair' thrown forward triumphantly, this specimen occupies prime exhibition space otherwise dominated by the owner's extensive modern-art collection. So arresting is the tree that you follow it instinctively with your eyes while traversing the first-floor ramp, which hugs the courtyard.

Cinematic sequences and the Corbusian concept of the architectural promenade come to mind as you view the feature tree, in its pebble garden, from different angles, framed by horizontal and trapezoidal windows. The continuous opening also allows much of the art to be illuminated by even, natural light.

Not surprisingly, the prized tree is on the 'special side' of three bedrooms, as Matin puts it: the guest bedroom looks directly at the courtyard, and the side-by-side bedrooms experience it as a backdrop.

Designed for the owner's now grown-up children (the house took five years to complete), the pair of mirror-image rooms is shielded by a honeycomb brick wall and double-glazed windows on the side facing the main road (the same can be found in the long master suite, on the same level). On the other side, the children's rooms open on to a shared balcony with built-in seating beside lemongrass plots resembling paddy fields. 'I don't want you to be here and to feel like you're on the second floor,' says Matin, sitting beneath the sky and enjoying the breeze rustling the leaves.

The rooftop affords a more encompassing sensation. Reached after navigating a ramp junction ('architecture at a crossroads', Matin jokes), the grassy uncovered roof area might feel like a road-level garden were it not for the gabled roofs of neighbouring houses peeping over creeper-covered perimeter walls. In front, however, the tops of tall, leafy trees specially planted within the compound and beyond feel as though they are but an arm's length from the shallow infinity ponds on the roof's edge. A copse forms the horizon, obscuring all but a skyscraper in the distance.

Up here you feel immersed in a widescreen-cinema experience, albeit with your feet firmly planted on the ground. Past the lawn and water barrier are fields of green. 'This is the ground floor,' Matin says, smiling. 'But downstairs is also the ground floor.

'It's all the ground floor.'

Above: Custom-made, painted bricks clad the house and help absorb traffic noise.

Pages 20–21: The ramp is flanked by the courtyard and a cubicle wall of art.

Opposite: A scenic corridor on the bedroom floor takes in a pond and the courtyard on the level below.

Right: Trees outside the house provide leafy vistas through street-facing windows.

Above: Perforated-brick exteriors hide and ventilate street-facing bedrooms.

Right: The Medusa-like mane of the feature tree provides a dramatic backdrop to the guest bedroom.

Above: Andra Matin jokingly refers to the meeting of the staircase and ramps as 'architecture at a crossroads'.

Right: The basement is illuminated by natural light infiltrating the grille between the courtyard and living areas above.

MARBLE HOUSE

Openbox Architects

BANGKOK, THAILAND, 2017

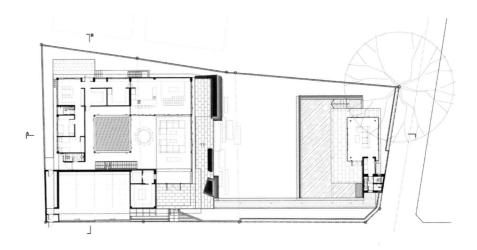

Marble House, in Bangkok, is divine.

That is the feeling it imparts, and for good reason. Feng shui consultants chose the building's position after locating an energy line that limited its footprint to only half of its plot. The propitious calculation, however, sent Openbox Architects back to square one, literally.

'Pushing back the buildable area gave us a square,' says Openbox co-founder Nui Ratiwat Suwannatrai. 'But square plans are not the most suitable for a tropical region; we had to find a way to make the building slim.'

The Thai architects had originally proposed a one-room-deep linear house to facilitate natural ventilation and lighting, requests from clients who had grown tired of air conditioning and artificial illumination. Having lived in a condominium nearby, the couple wanted the 'opposite' of everything apartment living entailed. That also meant raising their two young children in a home with a garden.

Before coming up with a new design, Openbox had to rethink one other challenge facing the 560-square-metre (6,030-sq-ft) plot

in an industrial area. Apart from a magnificent rain tree at the opposite end, the only other visual relief, the architects realized, was directly overhead. By inserting a 6 x 6-metre (20 x 20-ft) courtyard into the middle of the house, plus four air wells on the first floor, the family would have their own pieces of sky.

'We call this a private sky because surrounding the house are taller buildings and factories,' says Suwannatrai. 'Also, in the city at night, normally there is excessive glare when you look up. But when you frame the sky like this, you can enjoy it; you can see stars from inside the building.'

Not unlike the centrepiece of Jakarta's AN House (see pages 34–45), which allows the home to breathe, the courtyard at Marble House is contained within sliding glass panels, typically left open to ventilate surrounding spaces on two levels. Those include the vast living areas on the ground floor that spill on to the lawn, and, above the dining area, an open mezzanine hallway that doubles as a study. On the hottest days, a corner of the living room can be closed, limiting air conditioning to just

Opposite: Despite being surrounded by buildings, Marble House enjoys a high degree of privacy, even on the terraces attached to bedrooms on the top floor.

MARBLE HOUSE

Right: The owners like to
walk around the courtyard,
and expect the bamboo
to grow taller than the
house eventually.

Opposite, top: To lighten
the effect, marble
cladding was restricted
to the top floor.

Opposite, bottom: The
terrace off the main
bedroom looks as if it has
been carved from stone.

one side of the floor. The terraced courtyard, which steps downwards in concentric squares to a compact grove of black bamboo, cools the rest.

On the level above, freshness is bolstered in the en suite bathrooms by air wells that increase ventilation while also ensuring absolute privacy: look up at the bedrooms from the street and you are effectively stonewalled, your gaze going no further than the façade of what resembles an enormous sculpture. Windows, angled towards the garden, are contained within spaces that appear to have been excised by a giant chisel.

On the other side of the house, the main bedroom shelters behind a deep balcony seemingly also cut from marble. Its large, north-facing overhang is a tropical design strategy to enhance comfort.

So are the exterior large-format porcelain tiles, which help to keep the temperature down inside. This light, marble-printed cladding, affixed to brick walls to provide a second skin, was specified by Suwannatrai's clients, members of a family that sells construction materials. They wanted to use their house to test the panels' performance against sun and rain. 'They also wanted the house to make a statement,' says the architect.

There is a more fundamental reason for Marble House: the stone used to be an integral part of the family business and, fortuitously perhaps, falls under the earth element, lending feng shui advantages. That explains its extensive application outdoors as well as inside, where real marble, naturally cool because of its high heat conductivity, is used. The most obvious temperature moderator, however, is the central courtyard, kept damp to encourage the bamboo to reach for the sky.

Circumnavigating the void, Suwannatrai counts the many boxes that had to be ticked before Marble House could break ground. 'Its design is derived from all those restrictions,' he says.

The architects' achievements are written in stone.

Above: Stairs to the bedroom level have views of the bamboo as it rises through the house.

Opposite, top: The study-cum-television room is open to the living room below and to the courtyard.

Opposite, bottom: The courtyard is kept open to cool the dining and living areas.

MARBLE HOUSE

The faceted exterior
conceals bedroom
windows, angled
obliquely for privacy.

AN HOUSE
d-associates

JAKARTA, INDONESIA, 2017

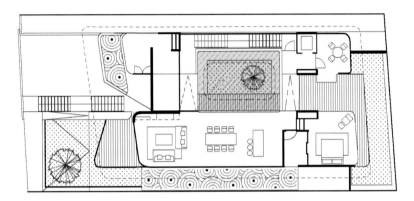

AN House has more reason than most to turn its back on the world. Like other courtyard houses with few or no windows inviting views in, it boasts a façade that allows life to take place away from the public gaze. However, while it may appear dark and defensive on the outside, it is bright and airy where it matters: behind its masculine, retro-modern exterior lies an open inner world.

Its high degree of comfort inside owes much to a central, 40-square-metre (430-sq-ft) courtyard. Two smaller voids contribute to natural lighting and ventilation, but it is the opening in the middle that is the mother lode. It also makes inward orientation possible.

Recent history was behind the design of the house, say d-associates' co-founders, Gregorius Supie Yolodi and Maria Rosantina. So were the forces of feng shui. Negative energy was the common link.

The T-junction position of the property, its owners worried, could block the flow of 'chi', resulting in pent-up universal energy that would disrupt the harmony if it found no release. To subvert the force, the architects

angled the building. 'We didn't want to get into an argument with the clients' feng shui guy so we avoided the sharp angles of the T-junction,' says Yolodi. 'Then we created curves to make the lines fluid and retro.'

More tangible concerns had to do with lingering ethnic tensions in Indonesia. In 1998 anti-Chinese riots left more than a thousand people dead. The nerve centre was a university campus near AN House where thousands of protesters had massed to demand the end of President Suharto's rule. Violence erupted after four students were shot dead.

From the deep, second-floor terrace of AN House, situated in one of Jakarta's Chinese enclaves, Yolodi points in the direction of the university where the tragedy unfolded. 'People are still worried, and their houses reflect that tension,' he says. 'Chinese people feel insecure in Jakarta.'

Also on the second floor, exterior walls in battleship grey vary in height, affording differing levels of privacy in the bedrooms and on the terrace. From this triangular outdoor area, the streetscape directly in front is

Opposite: A glass panel in front of the balcony doors allows a view of the rock garden by the main entrance below.

Left: Angling the house made the owners feel more comfortable about the plot's T-junction position.

Opposite, top: A bedroom, set back from the mouth of the house, extends on to a triangular balcony.

Opposite, bottom and pages 38–39: A wooden deck is part of the central courtyard, which provides air and light for the living areas and top-floor rooms.

presented cinematically in a continuous strip. At its entrance, glass lies beneath your feet, illuminating a minimalist water sculpture on the floor below. Above, a void perforates the roof.

Another cut-out accommodates a minor courtyard separating the master suite from a study. Tropical plants between them, flanked by windows beside desks, allow husband and wife to work in fresh air and in each other's company while inhabiting different rooms.

The real focus of the first and second floors, however, is the central courtyard, surrounded by sliding glass doors. Acting as the heart and lungs of the four-bedroom, 671-square-metre (7,222-sq-ft) house, the courtyard keeps the interiors fresh and breezy, aided by other openings: the living area, for example, merges with a terrace hidden from the street by a row of leafy tembusu trees. This same room can be opened to a long, narrow koi pond along its southwestern flank.

'Many Jakartans ask for air conditioning, but this house is comfortable without it,' says Rosantina. 'The units have been put in the bedrooms, just as options.'

'It's basic physics,' adds Yolodi. 'You have to create pressure differences in order to create

air circulation. The courtyard is one of the best ways of doing that.'

Different doors on different sides of the courtyard can be opened for varying wind effects, and kept that way at night.

On the top of the house, the three voids appear like a cluster of wells. In the middle, reaching for the sky, a eucalyptus tree will one day join the fruit trees on the roof garden. From here, Central Park Mall is visible, as are, unfortunately, excavations directly behind the house that presage high-rise towers. Ensuring privacy in this direction is a 12-metre-tall (39 ft) perimeter wall.

The gods should approve, because important rules have been met: as the feng shui consultant had instructed, the house does not extend all the way to the rear; the eucalypt is the sole tree in the main courtyard; and the front door is exactly where it should be.

'I say to our clients that feng shui is wind and water management,' says Yolodi. 'If you do good design, the house will have good air flow, good light; it will be good.' But he offers this suggestion if complaints about energy flow arise. 'Then,' he says, 'just find another feng shui guy.'

AN HOUSE

Above: A long, narrow pond runs alongside the kitchen, dining area and lounge.

Left: Desks in two rooms facing each other are separated by a leafy sitting area.

Left: A patch of sky is reflected on a curtain wall.

Below: The pond extends to the guest suite behind the kitchen.

Above: An elegant staircase climbs directly from foyer to bedrooms.

Opposite: At varying heights, the balcony wall controls views into and out of the house.

Right: A marble water feature is part of the minimalist rock garden.

Pages 44–45: Voids through the house resemble wells on the rooftop.

CABILDO RESIDENCE

CS Design Consultancy

METRO MANILA, PHILIPPINES, 2016

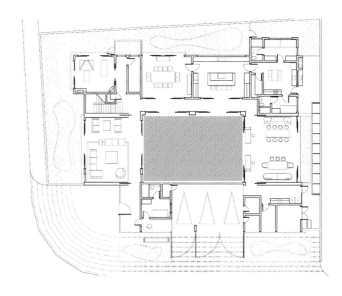

Among Metro Manila's gated communities, Urdaneta Village has the distinction of being closest to the business district. It is also invigorated by the green lungs of Urdaneta Park and Ayala Triangle Gardens. But despite owning a coveted address in this leafy, exclusive enclave, the Filipino clients of Anna Maria Sy faced challenges to their corner plot that can be explained in just four letters: EDSA. The Philippines' busiest highway, Epifanio de los Santos Avenue, hugs the perimeter of the village, conveying traffic but also one of its by-products – noise pollution.

Sy's design of a courtyard house for the family of three makes perfect sense in this context. Contained on all four sides, with a drop-off at the corner of the property, the home folds its arms against external commotion and sustains its occupants from within. At its core is a 103-square-metre (1,109-sq-ft) garden whose trees and shrubs provide visual if not acoustic buffering.

'The main part of the family's brief was that they wanted to minimize the noise,' says Sy, managing director of CS Design Consultancy.

'The whole idea of the courtyard was to have an enclosed area that felt detached from everything going on outside. It becomes a quiet inner space.'

Flat-roofed at the front, where it appears as a contemporary single-storey structure accommodating a three-car garage and an entrance around the corner, the house goes up a level at the back, where a pitched roof gives it a traditional feeling. Farthest away from the honking vehicles on EDSA are the bedrooms, including the master suite, which occupies an entire wing on the top floor. The L-shaped buildings of differing heights enclose the courtyard.

Because sound infiltrates buildings through their weakest acoustic points – windows being among the most vulnerable parts of walls – the use of double glazing was imperative, and its effects are instantaneous. Ears seem to pop and clear as you move from the front door straight into the formal sitting room, where framed views of the rectangular courtyard allow immediate engagement with the landscape.

Opposite, top: Hugging the courtyard, a corridor takes you from dining to entertainment rooms.

Opposite, bottom: The master suite above the entertainment room has the best view of the house.

CABILDO RESIDENCE

Opposite, top: Traditional with a contemporary twist, the house features a courtyard at its core and pocket gardens on its perimeter.

Opposite, bottom: The courtyard was envisaged as an inner sanctum detached from activity and noise.

Above: The entrance, by a corner drop-off, leads into the lounge and the U-shaped circuit around the courtyard.

Proceed along a corridor linking the rooms with the courtyard, and you reach the dining area, kitchen and finally a casual entertainment space. This area had been planned as a *lanai* (a Hawaiian term for a covered, open-sided veranda popular around the world, including in the Asia-Pacific), but heat and humidity made it sensible to have it enclosed and air conditioned when needed. From this end room, the formal lounge across the patch of green appears as an extension, and vice versa.

Acoustic considerations aside, the beauty of the courtyard's central placement lies in its ability to link people visually in different parts of the house. 'If you're sitting in the living room, you're looking right through it to rooms on the other side and it all feels like one large space, whether it's exterior or interior,' says Sy.

Bedrooms on the top level also enjoy through-views, from top to bottom and across the property, the best of which are from the master suite. In fact, save for the family area on that floor and the gym on the ground level, every room benefits visually from the courtyard.

Pocket gardens are part of the 1,013-square-metre (10,900-sq-ft) plot's planting scheme.

Greenery on either side of the rooms allows doors to be opened for an airing. By absorbing and scattering sound waves, the plants provide a measure of acoustic privacy and work in tandem with the physical barriers to attenuate traffic noise.

In reality, however, the courtyard is usually seen through glass – despite which, its owners insist, it is an integral part of the house. Having an internal garden, they add, means that enjoying the plants becomes a primary rather than an ancillary activity. The space may also become their child's private playground one day, taking the place of a nearby park.

So was the courtyard in fact successful as an architectural earplug? The answer must encompass more than simply the decibel-level drop owing to the plants and built-in sound barriers to highway hubbub. Simply put, the courtyard lends support psychologically.

'Just the fact that you are surrounded by an architectural volume creates an internal experience, away from the noise and congestion of EDSA,' says Sy. 'It makes you feel you're somehow far away from the traffic.'

Above: On the long side of the rectangular courtyard are the dining room and kitchen beside it.

Opposite, top: Double glazing, with the help of layers of plants in the middle of the property, reduces noise from a nearby highway.

Opposite, bottom: The dining room has a pocket garden on one side and a courtyard on the other.

PARAÑAQUE HOUSE
Atelier Sacha Cotture

METRO MANILA, PHILIPPINES, 2011

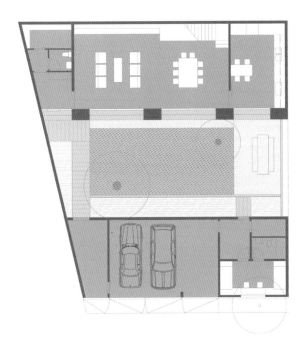

Make a wrong turn driving to Sacha Cotture's home in a gated community of Metro Manila and you might find yourself in Ethiopia, Finland or even Brazil. Although streets named after countries can confound first-time visitors to this 'multinational village', Cotture's courtyard house looks like no other residence around it, and not just because of its strong modernist lines. Unlike dwellings in this and other urban settings that are typically oriented towards the street, his family home presents an inscrutable front to the world.

'Some people thought it was a shop,' says Cotture about Parañaque House, built in 2011 and named after one of the cities that make up the country's capital region. 'Some thought it was a massage parlour.'

Such anonymity was integral to the courtyard house Cotture designed largely to create his 'own little world'. 'I always dreamed of having my own introverted space,' he says. 'And because the neighbourhood is not that attractive, the courtyard came quite naturally.'

Making the most of the 360-square-metre (3,875-sq-ft) plot he and his Filipina wife bought

as an investment – following a seven-year stint in Hong Kong that had inured them to tight living spaces – Parañaque House is organized in three roughly equal parts and extends to the plot's limits: the first slice is the single-storey garage, followed by the courtyard and then the three-level house. 'I liked having the house a bit of a distance from the street but still being able to look out,' says Cotture.

The entrance to the 450-square-metre (4,845-sq-ft) house leads from a concealed door by the garage, which has its own rooftop garden. Treated bamboo poles, stained and varnished, clad the street-side façade of this block, in addition to the top two floors of the house. Araal, a local granite of warm hues, adds weight to the ground floor.

The materials hint at a penchant for tradition and their application shares something with the courtyard typology once popular with the country's Spanish colonial masters – appreciated by Filipinos today, perhaps, but tied firmly to the past and uncommon in a contemporary context.

Opposite: A garden was planted on the roof of the garage, the back of which borders the courtyard.

'[Parañaque House] has no pretension to being vernacular architecture,' says Cotture. 'I'm just playing with some elements.'

The project was also Cotture's first in the Philippines, which may explain the romance behind his material choices. Otherwise, he stresses, the design was a given – he just needed to decide on proportions that would afford an internal garden as big and simple as possible.

To make this courtyard the focal point day and night, the speckled adobe-and-shell wall of the garage can be turned into a water feature, with lights. The living and dining areas make the most of this outdoor space, but it is also a visual treat for the areas that overlook it – three children's rooms and a play area a level up, as well as the parents' suite at the top, set back to control the building's scale. On one side of the courtyard garden is a *lanai* (a covered, open-sided veranda) leading from the kitchen. By the street entrance, on the opposite side, is a vine-covered walkway over a pond.

Interestingly, despite the courtyard's centrality, Cotture calls it 'a kind of false courtyard' because the open area backs on to the garage rather than being necklaced by rooms. But its enclosure – similar to those of hacienda courtyards bordered by buildings or walls – is absolute, and that is why it works for him.

Although the photographs of Parañaque House may show a manicured lawn, the reality is that it has become a rugged outdoor studio for Cotture. These days the architect-cum-artist expends his creative energy in his courtyard, producing 5-metre-long (16 ft) Chinese-ink paintings – several of which hang in luxury hotels. 'The introverted space is perfect,' he says. 'It is the perfect place to paint without being distracted by any exterior elements.'

Just as some courtyard houses lie beyond rigid definitions, so can they function in unexpected ways.

Above: A covered bridge, fringed with 'millionaire's vine', connects the street entrance to the bamboo-clad house.

Opposite: The parents' suite on the top floor is set back to control the scale of the building.

Left: The aim was to create an enclosed world that allowed indoor–outdoor living in safety and privacy.

Below: The kitchen extends on to the *lanai* at one end of the courtyard.

PARAÑAQUE HOUSE

Above: The entrance, which features araal stone and capiz shell, leads to a covered walkway above a pond.

Right: Bamboo cladding outside is complemented by bamboo poles affixed to the floating hardwood stairs.

Above: A capiz-shell chandelier and other tropical accents warm the courtyard-facing dining area.

Opposite, top: Beside the foyer is a large living area that merges with the courtyard.

Opposite, bottom: Coconut bark clads the feature wall in the main bedroom, which spans the top floor.

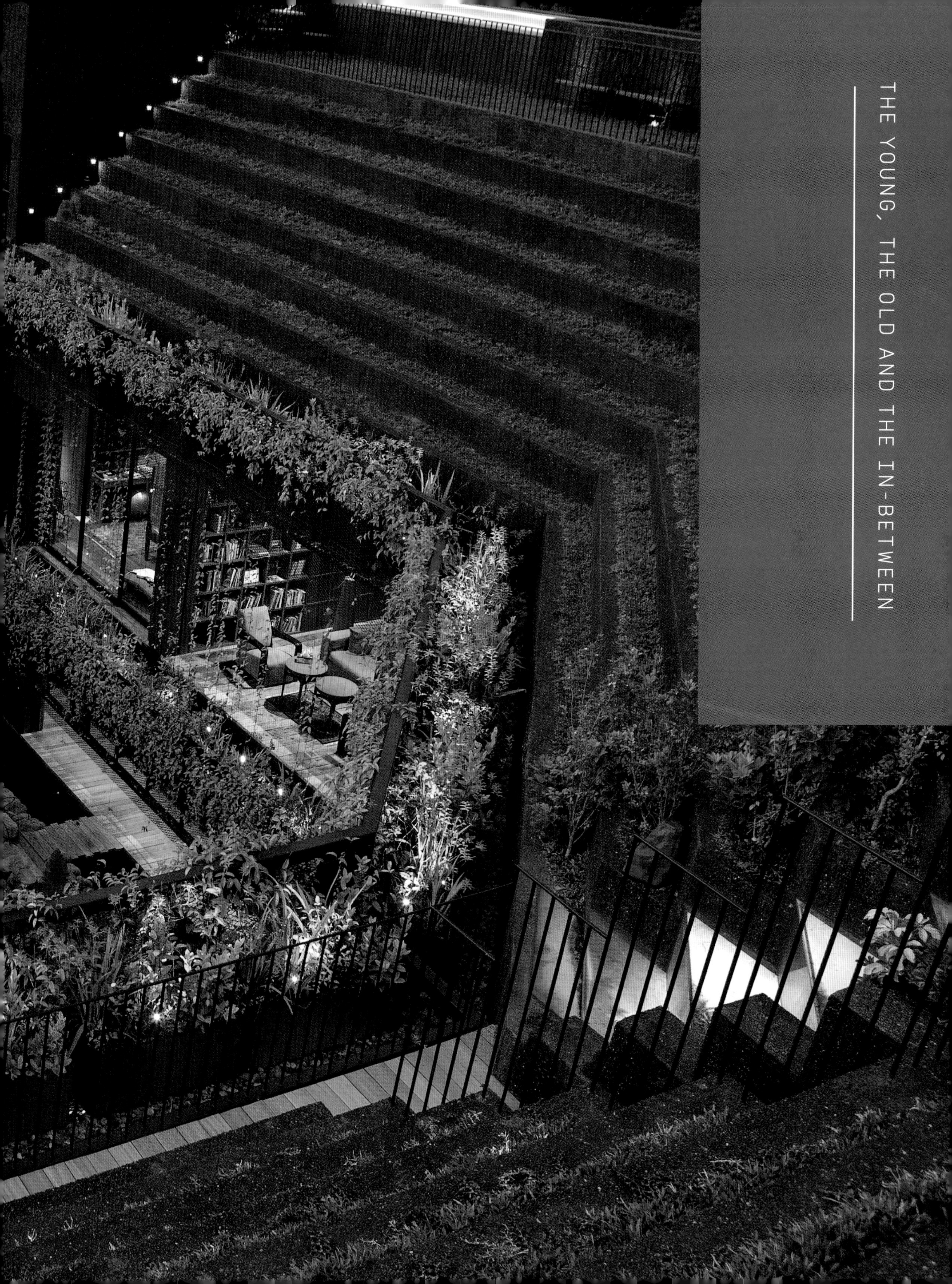

THE YOUNG, THE OLD AND THE IN-BETWEEN

The courtyards in the houses that follow allow extended families to live together under the same roof – an enduring ideal in many parts of Asia. One young Taiwanese architect borrowed directly from his cultural past for a modern-day response to the traditional Chinese courtyard house of his ancestors. Spatial divisions between public and private, plus a twenty-first-century hierarchy of rooms, make harmonious multigenerational living possible: the eldest members occupy the most convenient areas, while their children and respective families enjoy separate as well as shared spaces in and around a central courtyard. Similar was achieved at G House by mirroring a U-shaped dwelling to connect mother and son simply but effectively across a courtyard: a wall separates, while passages link, the two near-identical halves. At Cornwall Gardens a bridge was designed to bring young and old together symbolically and for good. This house, a tropical paradise centred on an idyllic courtyard pool, allows three or more generations to live in bliss. And who would ever want to leave that?

COURTYARD HOUSE

Dotze Architecture

CHANGHUA, 2014

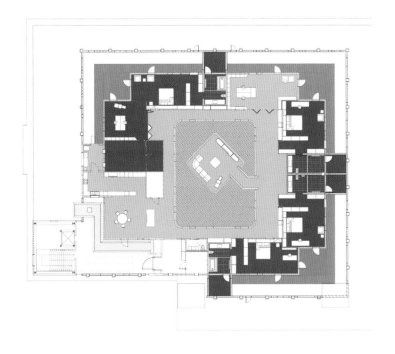

As social models go, intergenerational cohabitation attracts spirited and sustained applause. But the reality is that, increasingly, extended families remaining together by choice is the exception rather than the rule. Housing must share the blame.

Taiwanese architect Tze-Chun Wei, who has lived most of his life with his parents and siblings, points to a lack of buffer zones in modern homes as a reason for the atomization of families. Now married and a father of two, he and five other adult Weis reside in a home designed for the twenty-first century but inspired by thousands of years of tradition. His contemporary version of a Chinese courtyard house enables three generations to share space while leading individual lives – thus embracing the Confucian family ideal of old, young and in-between under one roof.

It helped that they did not have far to move. Instead of acquiring a residential plot close to the family's hosiery business they built on the roof of their single-storey factory. Access to the 662-square-metre (7,125-sq-ft) house, via a lift or staircase, is from a private

corner of the long industrial building. Away from the workers' entrance and parking, that section of the factory had been their home for decades.

Until they moved up, literally, the family inhabited three rooms behind the office. 'There was no natural light, and internal walls were just plywood partitions that didn't reach the ceiling,' says Wei. 'Our lives were tied to the factory.'

When it came to designing his family's new home, Wei, of Dotze Architecture, therefore considered how best to create a cool, quiet dwelling filled with natural light, yet shielded from public scrutiny. Internal views would shift the focus inwards.

Private areas were important, of course, but so were shared zones and family space. These different considerations led to a roughly doughnut-shaped house with a 158-square-metre (1,700-sq-ft) courtyard in the middle. A looped corridor connects individual units, while small 'sky voids' at the corners of the building separate them. Protecting the entire house is a perimeter blockwork wall, perforated for controlled views in all directions.

Pages 60–61: Flora and water combine at Cornwall Gardens, Singapore, for feel-good potency (see pages 82–93).

Opposite: Especially in rural areas, which lack parks and other public spaces, homes should also be playgrounds, says Taiwanese architect Tze-Chun Wei, seen here with his family in their central courtyard.

COURTYARD HOUSE

As in the Chinese quadrangle houses of yore, hierarchy lay behind the assignment of space. But where ancient codes would have placed senior family members in the structure furthest from the entrance (rear rooms being the most secure), in the Wei residence other factors were more important.

'My parents wanted to be close to the kitchen and entrance,' says Wei, adding that positioning their three-room suite as requested allowed the three siblings to occupy the opposite end of the house, each side enjoying its own living area.

Activity-wise, however, the dining room, attached to the open kitchen, is the most important family space. 'We all eat together,' says Wei. 'That is a must.' So although the site for shared meals constitutes the heart of the house, the courtyard, accommodating the living room in a standalone cube, is the centre.

'The object', as Wei refers to the cube, and its placement at a 45-degree angle, solved concrete and conceptual problems. One was the contradiction inherent in the modern desire to live with greater transparency but also privacy. Another was a courtyard that would have felt too open, and thus insecure.

In the cube, measuring 6 x 6 x 3.8 metres (20 x 20 x 12 ft), with windows bisecting the volume in a horizontal band at eye level, you feel as though you're on an observation deck. The position of the entrance suggests a communal area shared by all the siblings but, in reality, it is used mostly by Wei's brother and sister only. Wei and his family relax in the work-and-television room beside their bedroom, and his parents in the reading section of their suite.

With the placement of the living room in the courtyard, through-views across the square are obstructed but not completely blocked. Not being a hub of activity, it is also bare, save for a potted tree and a few pieces of furniture. 'My dad likes emptiness, so we kept it empty,' says Wei.

Other discussions between father and son clarified the meaning of courtyards and what Wei senior, who had grown up in a Chinese courtyard house in the area, wanted from the new family home.

'Courtyards represent gathering – of people, the air, the sun,' says Wei. 'Everyone had their own building [in his father's old house] but they felt like they were living under the same roof, and that has symbolic meaning. It means you are one family.'

As with the Chinese courtyard houses of antiquity, separation and connection were crucial to building togetherness in this family home.

Above: The Wei-family courtyard house stands on the roof of their stocking factory.

Opposite, top: A corridor leads to the courtyard cube, which houses the living room.

Opposite, bottom: The pond is by the entrance for auspicious reasons.

Pages 68–69: The courtyard greets you from every room.

Above and right: The entrance corridor takes you by the kitchen to the foyer, where the central courtyard comes into full view.

Opposite: In the living room, windows vary in size according to privacy needs.

Above: An outer wall obscures the bedrooms, with strategically placed windows affording edited views. Alongside walled-off sections connected to bathrooms, buffer zones also provide private outdoor areas.

Opposite, top: The dining room is positioned by an entrance corridor, so family members feel welcomed coming home for meals.

Opposite, bottom: 'My dad likes emptiness,' says Tze-Chun Wei.

FICUS HOUSE

Hatterwan Architects and Zarch Collaboratives

SINGAPORE, 2015

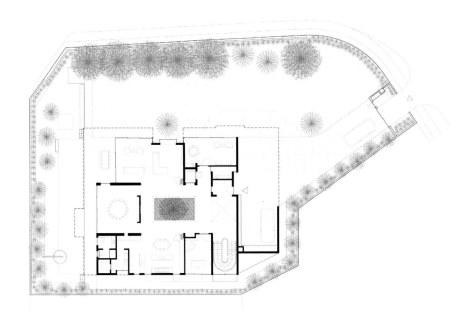

Architect Randy Chan will never forget the arrival of the eponymous ficus tree at this courtyard house in Singapore. 'It was like a bride coming into a new home,' he says. 'It took fourteen men to bring her in.'

Six metres (20 ft) tall and chosen as carefully as one might a spouse, the tree had beaten stiff competition to claim its spot in the middle of the five-bedroom house, designed by London-based Hatterwan Architects and Chan's Zarch Collaboratives to accommodate a three-generation family. Sited on its own island in a shallow pool open to the sky, the *Ficus benjamina* is so integral to Ficus House that, jokes Chan, 'The house is just a massive planter box.'

It is not difficult to see what he means. Life in this 1,460-square-metre (15,715-sq-ft) house, moments from Singapore Botanic Gardens, literally revolves around the courtyard and its tree, an axis mundi connecting earth and sky. Rooms on the ground and first floors are arranged in a rectangle around the 6 x 4-metre (20 x 13-ft) centrepiece. And directly below, in a basement as large as the footprint of the level above, light penetrating a gap in the floor plane

of the courtyard bathes the walls of what is essentially a giant travertine plant pot. The roots of the ficus, bound to restrict their growth, are contained within its stone barriers reaching the earth.

Typical of many courtyard houses in the Lion City – which sweats throughout the year when it is not swimming in rain – the void at the centre acts as an air shaft and a light well. The heart of the house, massed in two symmetrical volumes with a central articulated space, also affords an immediate connection with nature: birds nest in the branches of the ficus and their chicks take flying lessons indoors. Then there's the accompanying sense of well-being, say its owners.

That knock-on effect became apparent not long after they moved in. Because of forest fires in neighbouring Indonesia that closed schools for weeks in 2015, many in the city-state donned masks outdoors and, at home, shuttered windows and switched on air conditioning. Ficus House, however, remained open to the elements, even though the courtyard, with its atrium-like retractable roof

Opposite: The acrylic base of the water feature, housing the all-important ficus tree, allows light into the floor below.

FICUS HOUSE

Right: The heart of the house, the ficus tree is visible also from the top floor, which accommodates the bedrooms.

Opposite: The courtyard features a wall of concrete blocks positioned at different angles for a waterfall effect.

at the top, could have been closed. Although the tree had not been put in as a green filter, the owners believe it worked indirectly to mitigate the discomfort caused by air pollution.

'Courtyards came into being in Singapore to bring climatic comfort,' says Chan. But he fears that the recurring forest fires, together with extreme rainfall, will work against the already niche appeal of courtyard homes.

At Ficus House, a subtle strategy keeping the rain in check is an opening at the top of the void that is smaller than its base. In addition, blinds can be deployed to direct water into the proper channels, thus minimizing splashing on to the marble floor. Otherwise, rain is allowed simply to fall into the pool.

'It's nice to wash the tree,' says Chan, adding that the open kitchen – and the dining table providing what feels like front-row seating before its branches – is where the family tends to congregate.

It is on this floor that the openness afforded by the courtyard – and the way it connects all the spaces – is most apparent. The living area, opposite the kitchen, also segues into a shaded outdoor spot before a clear-sided swimming pool. Elsewhere on this level is a formal dining area, plus a study and private sitting room. A sweeping spiral staircase and a lift link the floors, as do the courtyard and tree, offering congenial family living in abundance. There

are ample opportunities to be on the private, bedroom level but in tune with activity on the ground floor. From the shower of one of the en suite bathrooms, peep holes in a feature brick wall allow sneaky views of goings-on below.

The design also includes familiar aspects of Singapore's black-and-white bungalows. These are the airily comfortable traditional houses with deep verandas that started appearing in affluent enclaves in the late nineteenth century. In Ficus House, the grand gestures of these colonial holdovers – which the clients referenced in their brief – translated into capacious rooms with high ceilings, balconies and wide eaves providing shade.

The house was also designed to meet the stringent standards governing Singapore's thirty-nine 'Good Class Bungalow' areas, where the minimum plot size is 1,400 square metres (15,070 sq ft). Among other regulations, including greenery stipulations, is a maximum building-site coverage of 35 per cent – something the courtyard, not part of the footprint, was able to expand visually.

But this courtyard would not be what it is without its defining element. 'We wanted a tree with character and we liked the ficus because it is romantic and poetic,' says Chan. More practically, he adds, 'It's an ordering device. Every view of it leads you back to the courtyard.'

Above, left: To manage rainfall, the void is smaller at the top than at the bottom.

Above, right: Acrylic was also used for the sides of the swimming pool.

Opposite: A few glass blocks in the feature wall allow a visual connection to the courtyard.

FICUS HOUSE

Opposite, top: Light from above bathes the sides of the tree's enormous travertine 'pot'.

Opposite, bottom: A window to the pool naturally lights the entertainment room in the basement.

Right: Ficus House is a twenty-first-century interpretation of a traditional black-and-white house.

CORNWALL GARDENS
Chang Architects

SINGAPORE, 2015

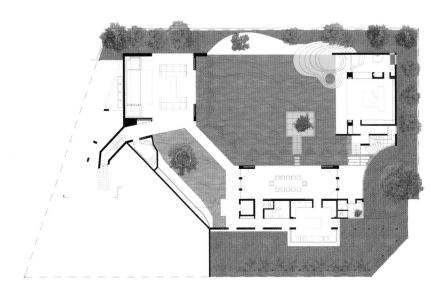

Not content simply with being a Garden City, Singapore now aims to become a City in a Garden, and Cornwall Gardens embraces the concept wholeheartedly. Designed by Chang Yong Ter of Chang Architects, the redeveloped home is a response to the owner's desire to use greenery and water to create a 'cool tropical paradise'.

That translates into a water-courtyard house, incorporating ideas that have evolved from Chang's previous experiments with landscapes in houses and, by extension, wellness through design.

Cornwall Gardens allows four generations of a family to live with flora, around a large pool. A roof garden and vegetable veranda, as well as planters and green walls, all bring life to this house on a 1,494-square-metre (16,080-sq-ft) plot. Adding charm and privacy are a mesh wall encouraging vines to proliferate, and vertical 'blinds' made up of creepers trained on cables. 'In the tropics these are also ways to cut down the glare,' says Chang.

Designing a courtyard house was not the aim, though, he adds. Instead, Cornwall

Gardens is the fulfilment of a desire to achieve 'oneness with nature'. In this home, recycled materials (wood, rebars) and old keepsakes (light fittings, window panels) sit easily with the new and lavish in a palette of subdued hues and tactile textures.

Past the façade – clad with charred logs, which filter air and sound – is a tropical idyll centred on 'the great outdoor space', which, says Chang, is always at the heart of a courtyard house. Positioning the rock- and palm-fringed pool in the middle allows interconnection among the rooms and full appreciation of its beauty. All six bedrooms and communal zones – the dining area, library and lounge among them – feel like box seats on Centre Court.

In a house built to accommodate many, it is no wonder the sofa is big enough for twenty people. Formal and informal supplementary seating can also be found in a fruit garden on the rooftop, on the terraces and even in the pool, where a sunken area comes complete with a longan tree.

Allowing young and old to live together, and encouraging future generations to want

Opposite: The greenery includes a longan tree in the pool lounge, and vines trained on wires in front of windows for shade and privacy.

Complementing the
house façade, clad in
charred wood, are details
such as doors made from
old railway sleepers and
a sculpted handrail
created from rebars.

Above: Shaded outdoor
sitting areas make the
most of the greenery.

Pages 86–87: The client
wanted the house to be
a 'cool, tropical paradise'.

to stay, motivated Chang's client to redevelop an existing house on the undulating site. Like Ficus House (see pages 74–81), the 1,300-square-metre (13,990-sq-ft) home falls into the Good Class Bungalow category, which limits building height to two storeys, although basements and an attic are allowed.

From its original L shape with pitched roof, the house expanded into a U configuration, with a double-storey 'planter bridge' – resembling an old railway line – linking the ends. 'Symbolically it connects the older and younger generations,' says Chang, pointing to bedrooms at either end.

The courtyard setup allows rooms around it to be lit and cooled naturally, aided by skylights and the terraced roof. And although everyone overlooks water, no one is closer than the client's son, whose bed, sunk into the floor, is at the same level as the pool and jacuzzi. Slide open the doors fronting his room and you're at the water's edge.

The abundance of moving water in this house is therapeutic, Chang believes, saying the eldest inhabitants especially have benefited from the mood-enhancing negative ions typically found near waterfalls and in oceans. A koi pond and triple-height waterfall ensure no shortage of feel-good molecules.

The sound of falling water – better than any piped music – is immediately apparent upon entering the house. In the dim coolness of the foyer, the plant-filtered light draws visitors to the pool below.

'To some people Cornwall Gardens is just about having a lot of greenery,' says Chang. 'But it is very much about nature integrated into living spaces, which the whole family share.'

There is definitely something in the air. The plants feel it too.

Above: The original
L-shaped house
was extended into a
U configuration, with
a bridge connecting
the ends.

Opposite: Bedrooms face
the swimming pool at
opposite ends.

Above, left and right:
Natural hues and dark
shades reduce glare
throughout the house,
including around the patio
and in bathrooms.

Opposite, top: Old mixes
with new in a landscape
teeming with life.

Opposite, bottom: Near
a pool-facing study
is the bridge, which
metaphorically links young
and old family members.

Opposite: A rooftop garden is intended for picnics and barbecues.

Right: Resembling an old railway line, the bridge connects two bedrooms on opposite sides of the U-shaped house.

G HOUSE

ar + d

BALI, INDONESIA, 2013

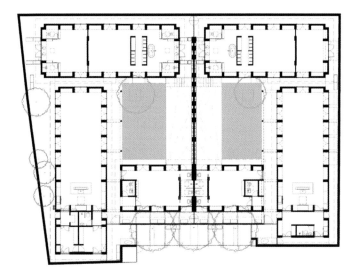

Stepping into Guraish Aldjufrie's home in Seminyak, Bali, is like leaving the tropical island behind at the threshold. Beyond the entrance, the mayhem of the upmarket commercial district vanishes as one is transported into a cool, contemporary refuge.

Although G House may not immediately reflect its surroundings, aspects of its design are deeply rooted in Asia. It is also grafted with cross-cultural references – much like its owner, a businessman of Indonesian, Arabic and Dutch heritage who lived in Los Angeles and Jakarta before settling in Bali more than fifteen years ago.

A repeat client of architect Ali Reda, of ar + d, Aldjufrie had, while in the Indonesian capital, developed an affinity for home life centred on the veranda. 'He'd lived around a *lanai* [a roofed, open-air porch] with large covered areas between inside and outside – where people sat and spent their time because nobody wanted to be in air conditioning,' Reda says.

Other factors, of course, helped to shape the house: the fact that Aldjufrie was planning to live there with his mother; his wish for a 'clean', urbane look; and the plot itself, whose distant sea views were likely to be lost to development. 'Even when we were constructing, those views were already being blocked by three- to four-storey buildings going up,' says Reda. 'It was a clear decision for us to try to afford Aldjufrie a little internal, private sanctum that he could spill out into and enjoy without being overlooked.'

Those objectives were achieved, in duplicate: G House is essentially two mirror-image his-and-hers homes wrapped around pools, and separated by a commanding stone wall. Each half consists of discrete single-storey pavilions of varying volumes. One accommodates the kitchen and living areas; another the en suite bedrooms; and a third the guest quarters, closest to the entrance, for easy access. A private, partially covered walkway connects the two sides on the 1,400-square-metre (15,070-sq-ft) compound's western periphery.

Within the walls, pavilions form the courtyards, with long living and dining spaces

Opposite: The plot, in a rapidly developing area, required controlled internal views.

94

G HOUSE

segueing into outdoor areas decked in ulin
wood. Cues, Reda says, came from Batavian
architecture and Singapore's colonial-era,
black-and-white houses, whose verandas ran
along the sides of the buildings to reduce heat
and glare inside. Crucial also to the comfort of
these traditional homes was cross ventilation.
Accordingly, the pavilions in G House are
one-room deep, ceilings high and openings
plentiful: taking the place of windows are floor-
to-ceiling timber-framed glass doors designed
to be held open to make best use of what Reda
calls the 'in-between space, under the pergola'.

While the courtyards' design takes ambient
temperature into consideration, the different
zones themselves – indoors, partially outside
and fully exposed – afford different levels of
protection from sun and rain. They bring to
mind, Reda says, a multifunctional jacket that
can be worn in different ways, morning, noon
and night.

The visual and experiential amenity of the
courtyards is clear in G House. So is the sense
of separation they engender, using the deck,
pool and wall: look up while outdoors and it's
the sky; to the side, and there's a 200-year-old
frangipani tree shedding shadows; behind you,
and there's the pergola; in front, and there's
the wall, acting as a sundial when light hits at
different angles.

'If it has to be an internal, controlled view,
then so be it,' says Reda, returning to the
reasons for his inward-looking design. 'There's
no use leaving garden space at the back or at
the side, or anywhere else you're going to be
struggling to get sun into and best use out of.'

The courtyards at G House, he adds, are
the best space 'in' the house: 'They're where
people can sit in silence if they want, sun on
their faces. Or where they can be in the shade,
cup of tea in the afternoon, and watch the
environment change.'

This page and opposite:
Five sets of doors, aligned
on opposite sides, are
kept open to ventilate the
living areas.

Pages 102–103: Similar tall
doors open the en suite
bathrooms and bedrooms
to the pools.

G HOUSE

ESSENTIAL SIGHTLINES

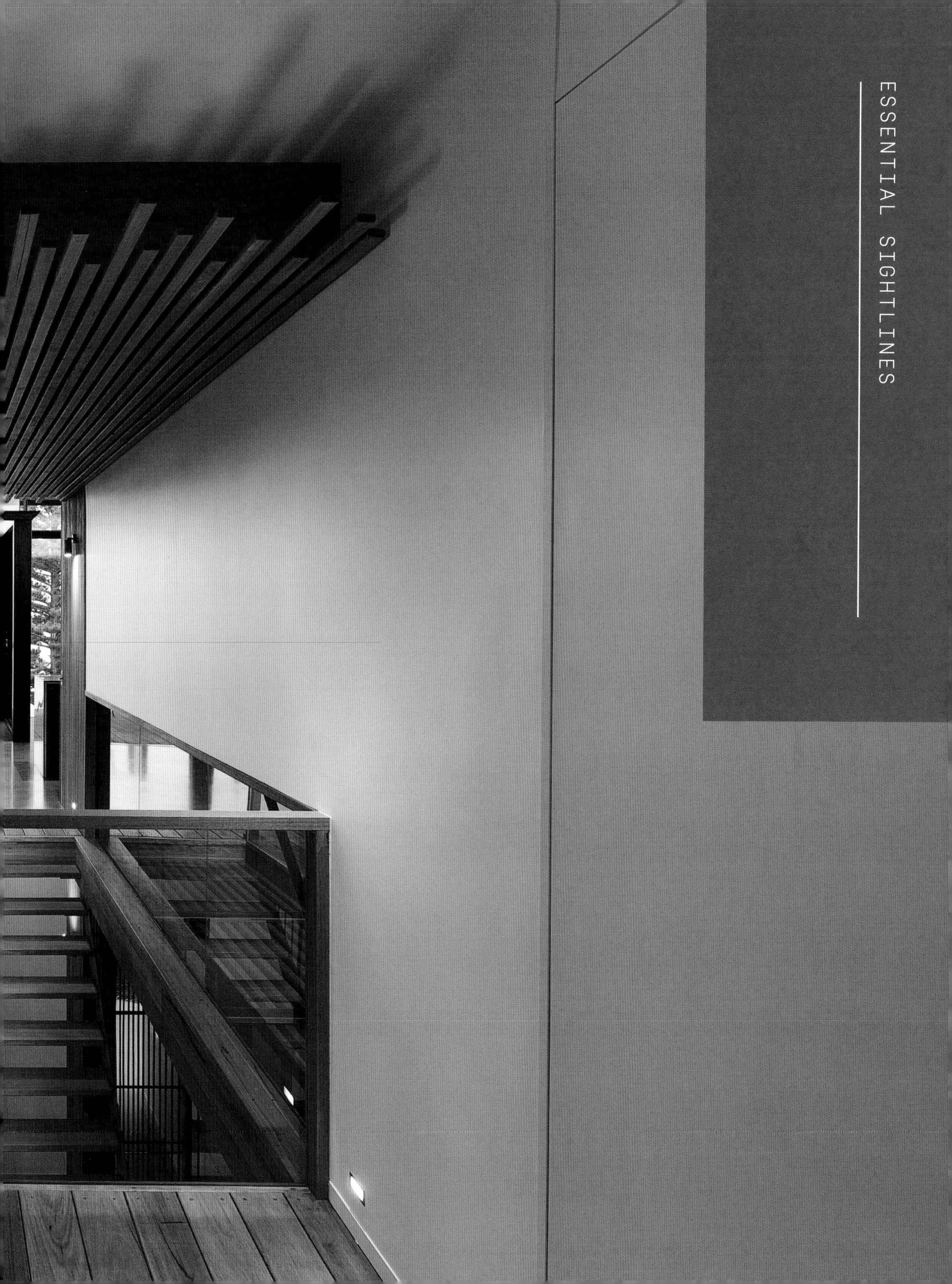

Imagine rooms linking hands across courtyards and then think of the see-through rewards those voids might confer. The houses in this chapter all benefit from sightlines that connect different parts of the houses in subtle or obvious ways. While courtyard houses often close themselves to the outside world and shift the focus wholly inwards, those with enviable vistas can take advantage of view corridors, which in a standard building might be difficult to achieve. The courtyards in Tyagarah and 2 + 2 House, while serving different functions, provide crucial visual links to the coast. Similarly, House by the Lake makes the most of its scenic location, its courtyard in the middle affording vantage points not only at the front of the building but also at the back. Residence Rabbits' courtyards reveal greenery at every turn, which was the primary goal. But they also offer transparency in ways that enhance interaction and bring the family closer together.

2 + 2 HOUSE
Matt Elkan Architect

SYDNEY, AUSTRALIA, 2016

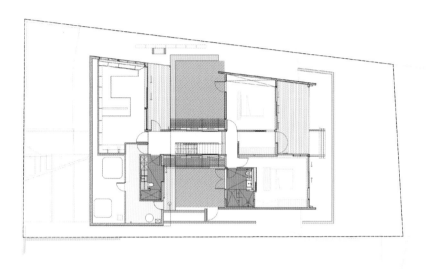

Prospect and refuge; public and private; rough and refined. Binary opposites in a home can find expression in multiple ways, but their importance lies fundamentally in balance. Such equilibrium underpins the pleasurable experiences designed into Matt Elkan Architect's 2 + 2 House, named after the 'wet' and 'dry' outdoor spaces separating two pavilions. In this beachside home, rooms capitalize on what are overwhelmingly the site's best attributes – but also turn their backs on those sea views.

The courtyards – which offer quiet, protected areas away from wild coastal winds – serve as the private, open-air leisure areas Elkan's clients wanted for themselves and friends. Idiosyncratically, perhaps, the couple chose not to exploit the vistas on both levels of the house, counterintuitively blocking much of the view from the lower floor of the rear pavilion for tantalizing glimpses instead. Creating altogether different environments in these green spaces – subdued foils for blue-water drama – proved too appealing to resist.

I know, because I was party to discussions focusing on the design of 2 + 2 House, my home in Sydney, Australia, and the catalyst for this book. The 'brave' move to carve out such inward-looking sanctuaries, as our architect described it at the time, would turn an otherwise simple design into something unexpected.

'Essentially what we've built is a double-banked-corridor conventional house, which is about the most efficient plan we can have,' says Elkan. 'Without really trying to, we've returned to a simple, symmetrical arrangement.'

The 250-square-metre (2,690-sq-ft) house, which hugs a steep slope down to a beach, is organized around a central axis beginning at the main entrance, on the top floor. A bridge connects the back pavilion to the front, to which a nose-like whale-watching platform is appended. On either side of the walkway, courtyards naturally lend light and air to the rooms adjoining them and give the house its H-shaped plan.

'In pulling the two halves of the house apart and creating a space in the middle we've kicked about five goals in one move,'

Pages 104–105: View corridors make the most of the beachside location of 2 + 2 House.

Opposite: The 'wet' courtyard contrasts with its 'dry' counterpart on the other side of the staircase.

says Elkan. That included achieving privacy in the courtyards and connection elsewhere: being able to walk around the house and look across to someone on the other side is a bonus.

Intentionally room-sized, the wet and dry courtyards segue from internal spaces catering to different traffic. Their Janus-faced juxtaposition, however, is partly the result of bearing: the dry courtyard, facing north, is the sunny outdoor living area connected to a library accommodating not just books but also a kitchenette and sofas; its southern, wet counterpart, yin to the other's yang, is home to ferns and a pond. The more intimate of the two, this shady courtyard extends from two bathrooms and is intended for family use only. That contrasts with the library and its courtyard, both stops on the guest route. From the open living areas on the top floor, the staircase is oriented towards this communal area. A covered deck and an outdoor, L-shaped concrete bench near the barbecue promise al fresco meals in a sheltered environment all year around. Walls on three sides, plus bamboo along a perimeter fence, bound the courtyard.

While the exterior spaces impart a sense of security and satisfy the physical aspects often attributed to courtyards, their success also lies in not feeling overly confining. 'A house that is too much about prospect and not about refuge means you sort of feel like you live on the edge of a cliff,' says Elkan. 'A house that is too much about refuge and not enough about prospect hems you in.'

Upstairs and down, from unobstructed vistas of the Pacific to flashes of water through view corridors, every room retains a visual link to the coast, and that owes much to the courtyards. The view backwards, or downwards, into these outdoor spaces is also a plus. Although neither courtyard is directly accessible from the main living room, they are important when seen as cubes of space enclosed by the building. Without the positive space to look through, the living area becomes a different room.

'The site is entirely driven by prospect,' says Elkan. 'But you don't want to be on show all the time and exposed to weather all the time, so physically, thermally and emotionally you need to retreat.'

Our courtyards provide the requisite haven.

Above, left and right: A granny flat overlooks the dry courtyard and, on the other side, opens on to a garden.

Opposite: The entrance pavilion presents an inscrutable face to the street.

Opposite: Stairs off the
living areas lead down
to the library and two
courtyards. Doubling
back below the bridge,
one reaches the main
bedrooms and
a bathroom.

Below: Hunkered into
the landscape, the library
is a multifunctional area
that can be opened to
the dry courtyard even on
windy days. Water views
add to this protected
outdoor 'room'.

Left: The wet courtyard, the more private of the two outdoor areas in the middle of the house, features a pond and a shower.

Below and opposite: At the far end of the wooden bridge, a pivot door leads on to a whale-watching platform, named for the humpbacks that ply the waters.

2 + 2 HOUSE

Flanking the bridge are the two courtyards, visible from full-height louvres and a low, horizontal window. The courtyards can also be seen from the kitchen and a concrete bench in the lounge.

RESIDENCE RABBITS

Boon Design

BANGKOK, THAILAND, 2017

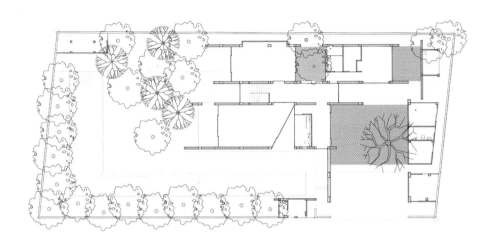

'Be formless, shapeless, like water,' martial arts maestro Bruce Lee once said. 'You put water in a cup, it becomes the cup. You put water into a bottle, it becomes the bottle. You put it in a teapot, it becomes the teapot.'

Those pearls of wisdom so resonated with leading Thai landscape architect Pok Kobkongsanti, of TROP, that he strung them into his own work. He says: 'When I founded my own company [in 2007] I thought I had to develop my own signature design. But the more I tried the worse the result, because I forced the design on to the site with no context. Then I found that ["Be Water"] clip.'

Bangkok-based architect Boonlert Hemvijitraphan, of Boon Design, helped Kobkongsanti go with the flow in creating Residence Rabbits (named after Kobkongsanti's Chinese zodiac animal). The two-and-a-half-storey, three-bedroom house occupies a 1,200-square-metre (12,915-sq-ft) plot in the Thai capital.

Key to the design are four main walls. Rather than forming a box, these partitions run parallel to each other, on an east–west axis, with rooms and voids integrated in between. The house thus met the brief for a series of courtyards that allowed indoors and outdoors to be enjoyed 'at the same time'.

No mere throwaway line from Hemvijitraphan about bringing the outdoors in, that stipulation also refers to the ways in which the courtyards mediate between the environments. 'The in-between spaces create an endless series of complex connections in a simple house,' the architect says.

The first courtyard greets you even before you enter the house, built on former swampland that has been elevated to protect against flooding. Facing you as you drive into the garage, the courtyard is an enchanting landscape of pompom hedges and dill thickets around mature trees, transplanted on the house's completion in 2017. This outdoor area, bounded by a standalone helper's quarters at one end, is a living gallery whose sculptural exhibits can also be viewed from the foyer as well as from Kobkongsanti's study, a level above.

In fact, greenery in this house greets you at every turn, through large glass panels or

Opposite: The trees in the main courtyard embellish the minimalist kitchen and a study on the first floor.

The main courtyard,
a private sitting-out area
beneath trees, can also
be appreciated from
a corridor near the foyer.

5.5-metre-tall (18 ft) sliding doors that open the rooms at opposite ends. In another captured space, between the double-volume dining/kitchen area and a ground-floor guest bedroom, wooden decking defines a sitting area shaded by trees. These also provide a leafy outlook for the client's wife, Romanee, a writer and illustrator whose study above feels like an airy room in a contemporary tree house.

'My courtyards are about how to deal with Bangkok's extreme climate, which is very hot,' says Kobkongsanti. 'We have tried to create a microclimate to reduce the temperature by at least a few degrees compared with the road in front of the house.'

Like the trees, tall exterior side walls cool the 420-square-metre (4,520-sq-ft) house and provide privacy. A small break in the southern expanse opens to a triangle sliced from the back of the lounge. This void offers similar benefits to the two courtyards, also bringing light and air to Kobkongsanti's office. Although not strictly a courtyard (it is covered, for one thing), the wedge is an indelible part of a sequence of liminal spaces that lend the house transparency where it is useful: views of the

living areas are possible from the two studies and from passages leading to the bedrooms on the top floor.

Then there's the fourth enclosure, an 'edible garden' of herbs tucked between the laundry and the spare room. The most private of the courtyards, it ensures that guests, too, wake up to greenery.

'Courtyards are everywhere in our home,' says Kobkongsanti, whose love of them does not mean, however, that he or his family enjoy them the way they do their garden. There, a 44-metre (144-ft), L-shaped pool encourages activity amid more than thirty trees planted along its outer sides and in front of the living areas.

'We cannot live without the courtyards now,' he insists, pointing to the luxuriant opening that enhances his wife's office, and the courtyard by the garage and foyer that invigorates him every day. 'I rarely use it, but it gives me energy in the morning when I leave and in the evening when I return. I didn't expect Boonlert to design a house like this.'

Somewhere, Bruce Lee must be smiling.

RESIDENCE RABBITS

Above: The courtyard
in front of the garage
provides uplifting parting
and welcome-home
views.

Right: Behind the walls of
the street entrance is the
L-shaped pool.

'Courtyards are everywhere in our home,' says landscape architect Pok Kobkongsanti, who wanted to integrate greenery into the rooms.

RESIDENCE RABBITS

Manicured hedges feature
in a courtyard serving the
garage and the foyer.

Opposite: A deck extends
from the dining area into
the garden.

Right: The owners love
being greeted by this leafy
view in the morning.

Pages 126–127: Rooms
have green views to the
east and west. The pool
dog-legs around to the
street entrance.

TYAGARAH

*Lisa Hochhauser,
Jan Hochhauser,
Drew Heath Architects*

BYRON BAY, AUSTRALIA, 2010

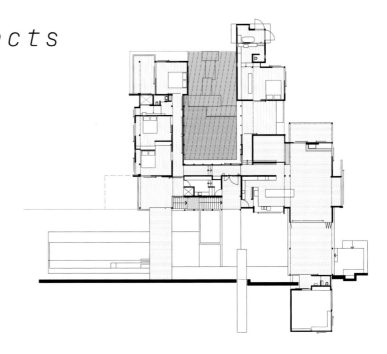

Tyagarah is possessed of the quiet kind of beauty that recalls Junichiro Tanizaki's think piece *In Praise of Shadows*. Timber-clad inside and out, filled with tribal artefacts and with a courtyard in the middle, the house underscores the timelessness of Tanizaki's 1933 essay on aesthetics, illuminating Japan's seemingly unique fondness for muted rooms with 'a sheen of antiquity'.

That Japanese essence becomes more persuasive the further one explores the house – although the story of its beginnings stretches back to a style of building far removed from the East.

In 1998 landscape architect Lisa Hochhauser, her husband, Robert Bleakley, and their three children decamped from Sydney to live on their 49-hectare (120-acre) Byron Bay property. An existing house, a 'Queenslander' by the road, served as a temporary home that would allow them to study the site to optimize its potential.

'We lived there and took our time,' Hochhauser says, explaining that, in preparation for their future house, she started

creating around it – amid boulders of basalt – a wonderland of tropical and rare plants.

It was clear where the house should be sited to make the most of 180-degree vistas extending across the hinterland to Australia's most easterly point, Cape Byron Lighthouse. Also apparent was that a courtyard in the middle would provide shelter from the punishing winds striking from all directions. The courtyard, she says, 'allows for views through and across while continuing to provide protection'.

Having worked out (in collaboration with her brother, US-based architect Jan Hochhauser) the floor plan, the composition of the house and how it sat on the site, she then sought a local counterpart who would finesse the details and bring to the project knowledge of materials available in Australia.

Enter courtyard enthusiast Drew Heath. The Sydney-based architect now credits his client with transforming his appreciation of gardens, and planting in him the concept of a house as only a small part of a greater landscape.

Another inspiration was Katsura Imperial Villa, Kyoto. Long applauded by modernists for

Opposite: The courtyard provides shelter when winds make it difficult to occupy other outdoor spaces.

its functionality and flexibility, the seventeenth-century exemplar of modular design provided ideas for the use of sliding panels to throw open rooms, and *engawa* corridors to layer space and provide the transition between outside and in. The Japanese cedar masterpiece, whose dark colours contrast with and draw attention to the bright hues of its extensive gardens, also moved Heath towards the Japanese tradition of post-and-beam construction.

Where originally Tyagarah had been conceived with greater use of concrete, more of a stepped terrace design and a curved roofline (replaced with a skillion roof), it evolved under Katsura's influence. 'We took the plan and overlaid Katsura on to it to set up a grid of posts and beams. Same plan, but, for me, a totally different building,' says Heath.

Among Tyagarah's highlights are the exposed structural elements. These appear as a ribbon of beams running around the 1,000-square-metre (10,760-sq-ft) floor plan (verandas making up 30 per cent of the figure) and overlapping in places to create a 'super-rigid structure'. They also emphasize the straight lines common to Japanese architecture.

Then there's the courtyard, which is suggestive of Japan not only in its understatement. On one side, tiers of sliding doors connect bedrooms with the garden, while on the other a veranda, open at opposite

Away from the intensity of the main view, a swimming pool shifts the focus to the garden.

ends, frames the view to the coast. The captured landscape organizes movement by employing wooden platforms to bridge the pavilions. They also step down the sloped plot towards an outdoor shower and beyond.

Opening the courtyard's northern boundary invited more of the garden into the house, says Lisa, recalling the initial, closed 'doughnut' configuration of the building. The revised C-shaped plan allowed not only greater integration of landscape with architecture but also external access.

Beside the house, a *Banksia* tree in the courtyard dapples a kidney-shaped pond accommodating grasses and lilies. 'It would be presumptuous to try to recreate a Japanese garden, unless you really understood the philosophy behind them,' says Lisa. But the nod to Japan is discernible.

Soft lighting plays a part. 'I like to work with layers of natural light and I particularly like reflected light off the floor surface, which in this case is planting,' says Heath. 'So you get this natural green light reflected into the corridor space and the bedrooms when they're open.'

Such illumination nudges Tanizaki into the open. 'Were it not for shadows,' he wrote a long time ago, 'there would be no beauty.'

TYAGARAH

Opposite, top, and right:
The courtyard extends
down a series of steps
and platforms.

Opposite, bottom:
Verandas, in every
direction, make up about
a third of the house.

133

TYAGARAH

Cape Byron Lighthouse, Australia's easternmost point, lies in the distance.

Above: Architect Drew Heath credits Kyoto's Katsura Imperial Villa with inspiring Tyagarah's post-and-beam construction.

Opposite: The overhanging roof, with corner flourishes, allows doors to be left open during rain.

HOUSE BY THE LAKE

Thisara Thanapathy Architects

COLOMBO, SRI LANKA, 2018

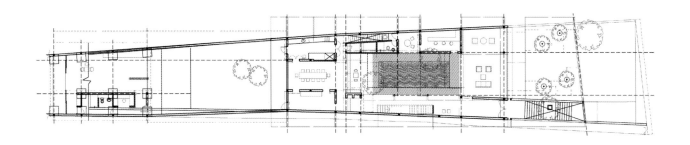

Architects have long understood the power of buildings to calm the mind. Temples and other places of worship often provide quiet spaces, as do public institutions including libraries and museums. Homes have also been designed in Asia and elsewhere to include prayer or meditation rooms for reflection.

Abeyratne House and the more recent House by the Lake, both in Colombo, were designed to foster detachment from the thinking process, but not necessarily by resorting to quiet nooks for respite. Instead, Sri Lankan architect Thisara Thanapathy conceived the houses wholly around introspection, so that inhabiting almost any part of them might produce what scientists suggest is architecture's measurable – and positive – effect on mental states: results of a 2014 US-based study showed that merely by viewing images of 'contemplative buildings' subjects entered into 'a meditative state with diminishing levels of anxiety'.[1]

Thanapathy believes that courtyards with clear boundaries, in addition to the right proportions and hence spatial quality, can achieve the same. A planted outdoor space inhabits the middle of Abeyratne House, which in 2011 won him the Geoffrey Bawa Award for Excellence in Architecture. The courtyard in House by the Lake, however, is a rectangular pool, contained to give it form in the centre of the house.

'My primary concern [with the lake house] was to create a very defined courtyard around the pool,' says Thanapathy, explaining why, for example, the bar area and kitchen to one side of it are walled off to form a clean, elongated expanse on the main floor. The minimalist aesthetic helps to keep mental clutter at bay: the only exposed elements are the lounge and dining areas at either end of the pool, and an internal rooftop garden of potted trees.

The feeling of enclosure fundamental to courtyards is further enhanced by slatted wooden screens along the top-floor corridor, which wraps around three sides of the courtyard. Sliced by shadows, the passage – outside the two bedrooms at the front of the house and two bedrooms at the rear – resembles a circuit for walking meditation.

Opposite: Trees shade the entrance stairway, which leads from road level to the front door.

HOUSE BY THE LAKE

Opposite and above: The pool courtyard is visible through the living room, which merges with a deep front garden that conceals the rooms from the road.

Pages 142–143: The walls of a poolside bar help bound the open space in the middle of the house.

Below, the turquoise pool circumscribed by grey, unembellished walls fixes the gaze.

Reflective bodies of water, often found at memorials and sanctuaries, metaphorically embody absence. The aim is to still the mind and focus on what's inside, says Thanapathy, adding: 'When you're looking inwards you're cut off from the rest of the world and you become silent.'

Restricting views of buildings flanking the property was important because removing distractions is key to creating a meditative space. Additionally, because windows on the main floor are in the closed-off kitchen and bar only, there is absolute privacy elsewhere.

Despite the courtyard concentrating attention at its core, the 678-square-metre (7,300-sq-ft) house also enjoys views of a lake. Capitalizing on this required hiding traffic along a road separating the property from the water's edge.

'We had to play with the levels when we designed the house, so that we cut off the road and you see just the lake,' says Thanapathy. Now, on the main level, the road is visible only

from the garden above the basement garage. So, from the living and dining areas (and the pool between them), it feels as though water may lap against the grass.

Lakeside breezes enhance this illusion. The house can be cooled naturally by opening the veranda doors at the front, allowing air to circulate through the void and out of the leeward end. As with traditional Sri Lankan courtyard houses, the feature's central position improves interior comfort not only through cross ventilation but also with light. Additionally, deep overhangs along the courtyard perimeter provide shade.

Thanapathy stresses that his urban courtyard houses are designed specifically to enable their inhabitants to switch off and enter a different world. The trees growing in the middle of Abeyratne House help to transport its owner to the countryside of his youth. The pool in House by the Lake is a similar portal.

'The courtyard calms you,' says Thanapathy. 'It gives you a different mindset.'

Above: From the living
room, the lake across the
road appears to extend
from the front garden.

Above, right: Slivers of light pattern the concrete floor of the timber-screened top-level passageway.

Right: The dining area has direct views of the back garden and, in the other direction, the nearby lake.

BRAMSTON RESIDENCE

KIRK

BRISBANE, AUSTRALIA, 2016

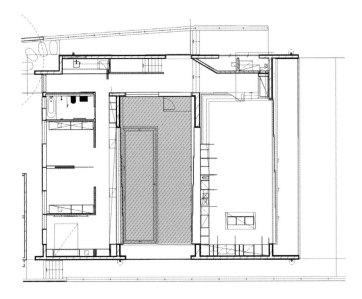

They may be fans of the typology now, but Michael and Anwen Batchelor – like many other homeowners interviewed for this book – did not stipulate that theirs should be a courtyard house. Instead, preliminary discussions with their architect centred on the site in question, how they wanted to use it, and the way they wished to live.

The ability to engage as fully as possible with nature was a requirement – typical for a young family of four in the capital of Australia's Sunshine State. The couple also wanted their new home to foster other kinds of connections, not just between themselves and their surroundings, but also with each other, effortlessly.

'The old house was tiny and we were always in the same space as each other,' says Michael, referring to the original cottage on the plot. And using the backyard was not without problems, remembers Anwen. Keeping an eye on the children outdoors was difficult if she was inside.

Teeming with established and newly planted trees, the sizeable backyard was itself a consideration: it abuts another of the Batchelors' properties, the two destined to become one in the future. Allowing for intimate and distant views was naturally important.

In ticking the boxes and producing a 'simple family house' on a sloping, 815-square-metre (8,770-sq-ft) plot on the outskirts of Brisbane, Richard Kirk came up with a model that, he says, can be adapted for other sites and offers a 'different' way of dealing with a suburban setting. At Bramston Residence the courtyard, as the main room in the middle of the house, is an integral part of a scheme of stepped terraces providing internal and external living spaces.

A common strategy in benign climates, the use of a thin building footprint allows for cross ventilation and natural light. The ability to view the captured section of landscape from most parts of the house meant also that the courtyard was the perfect spot for a pool. By not defaulting to the backyard, where suburban pools are often found, the Batchelors saved themselves from a lifetime of leaf-litter clean-up.

Opposite: Placing the pool in the courtyard instead of in the garden keeps it clear of leaves.

The house, consisting of two pavilions under a unifying roof, loosely separates private and public. A double-storey section accommodates parents on the top floor and children on the bottom, both levels overlooking the courtyard. Opposite, a tall, flexible, open-plan living, kitchen and dining area extends imperceptibly into the garden.

Sightlines made possible by the courtyard were multiplied and lengthened by the generous use of sliding glass panels that give new meaning to the term 'open house'. They allow all rooms to be visually linked, to each other as well as to the landscape. The visual axes also trick the eye, making the house feel larger than its 250 square metres (2,690 sq ft) of floor space.

It is an 'easy house to live in', the couple say, primarily because of the courtyard. 'From a practical point of view,' Anwen explains, 'it's easier to supervise the kids because I can be busy doing my thing and the kids can be in the pool.'

There was, however, an unanticipated drawback (apart from a glazing bill about a third of the cost of the entire house). 'It drives Michael crazy, but you can talk to anyone in any room of the house from anywhere,' Anwen jokes, her comment bringing to mind the direct channel for communication made possible by the void perforating a21 studio's multi-storey Saigon House (see pages 202–209).

However, in the Bramston Residence courtyard voices do not bounce off walls.

Outside the children's rooms is a long workbench with a view of the courtyard.

The enclosure relies on a full-height stainless-steel trellis to provide a green screen (creepers are planned) on the side open to a neighbour. The same wire mesh is used elsewhere in the house to comply with pool-safety regulations.

Looking back at the house from the lush garden, it is clear how the full-width openings allow for reciprocity, between the building and its landscape, created in the courtyard and preserved in the backyard. The absence of a deck abutting the living area further blurs the boundaries between the two. 'In Queensland everyone has a deck, but Richard [Kirk] said that as soon as you have an "outdoor area" you have an inside and an outside, and you replicate your indoor furniture outside,' says Anwen.

From the house, the green view takes in the old, majestic jacaranda that persuaded the couple to purchase the property. They have already started growing a candlenut tree, however, should it succumb to age.

Such future-proofing is part of a grand plan to redevelop the adjoining property. Not surprisingly, as with the Batchelors' first courtyard house, family and connection will be steering that discussion, alongside how landscape can be exploited for these and other purposes. 'This is my vision,' says Anwen. 'We're all around a central tree and a garden while having our own private space.'

Furniture in the living room can be rearranged to suit the family's needs.

Above: The top floor
accommodates the grown-ups.

Opposite: The courtyard's
centrality allows constant
supervision of the children
when they are in the pool.

Pages 152–153: Plants
are planned for the
courtyard's trellis window.

BRAMSTON RESIDENCE

Opposite: Plants trained
on wires serve as natural
screens for the bedrooms.

Above: This 'see-through'
house facilitates indoor–
outdoor and room-to-
room connections.

Deprive a house of its courtyard and life within turns dull and stuffy. That is because natural light and air are key elements of most courtyard houses. Take 17 Blair Road, in Singapore: gloomy and cocoon-like after its courtyard had been enclosed, the old shophouse was restored by owners sensitive to its original design and keen to minimize reliance on artificial comforts. Similarly, the owners of Saigon House saw sense in preserving the internal void in their 3-metre-wide [10 ft] house, slotted in between alley homes as dark as they are narrow and tall. In semi-subterranean houses that would otherwise gasp for breath at the back, excavated cavities make for dramatic vents and illumination. Rather than bathe its interiors in light, however, Shadow House was designed to keep everything cool. Orientation and deep overhangs helped, as did a womb-like pocket in the middle for ventilation. A further passive-design strategy channels breezes through the courtyard's constricted opening.

17 BLAIR ROAD

Ong&Ong

SINGAPORE, 2013

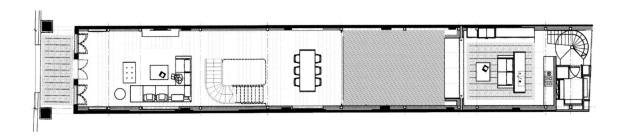

Singapore has manifold reminders of its founder, Sir Stamford Raffles, whose historical importance is underscored in the names of everything from landmarks to streets to businesses and even flora and fauna – the *Nepenthes rafflesiana* pitcher plant among them.

But the British statesman's legacy also lurks, unannounced, in the shadows of this former colony. In 1822 his was the directive that the city's shophouses have uniform fronts. Not only that, but they were to provide space 'open at all times as a continued and covered passage on each side of the street'. Thus was born the 'five-foot way', so called because of the minimum width allowing pedestrians to shelter from the elements as they went about their business.

These public thoroughfares are artefacts of times past, but walk across the veranda, beneath the ornate façade of this Ong&Ong-designed home on Blair Road, and you cross a threshold into the twenty-first century. Unlike many of the twenty-plus shophouses Maria Arango and Diego Molina have restored in the Lion City, this 450-square-metre

(4,845-sq-ft) dwelling – restored to reflect the Late Shophouse Style prevalent in Singapore from 1900 to 1930 – boasts an internal rectangular courtyard spanning the 5-metre (16-ft) width of the property.

But it was not always like this. In its former life as a converted warehouse, all the courtyard elements had been removed such that the ground floor was a single, continuous space stretching the entire length of the property, from street to alleyway. Little wonder the new owners chose to puncture the dark cocoon.

Though an important feature admitting light and air, the interior courtyard is allowed a certain flexibility by the city-state's Urban Redevelopment Authority, whose shophouse conservation guidelines are otherwise stringent. Arango and Molina say that owners are thus the ones determining size, shape and even if the space is to be roofed, which allows for all manner of layouts: Often the void is half the property's width, although sometimes it is only the size of a light well, and large shophouses may be segmented by several voids.

Pages 156–157: 3 Houses is squeezed on to an awkward site in Ho Chi Minh City, Vietnam (see pages 210–217).

Opposite: The courtyard separates the main building at 17 Blair Road from the double-height kitchen at the back.

Making the most of their unusually long plot, the French-Singaporean owners opted for a generous patch of green between their front and rear blocks. The space provides a safe playground for their two children in a park-poor area, and is a focal point of almost every room. From the entrance itself, your gaze is drawn through the main living area to the garden and beyond, underscoring, too, the role courtyards can play not only as the main source of illumination but also in creating magical spaces with alternating natural light.

The brightest indoor areas flank the courtyard and centre on family meals, which are taken in the double-volume kitchen of the back block, or, more formally, at the dining table in the front building. From these spots,

lushness confronts you horizontally and vertically, with the garden continuing up one of two party walls as the cohesive element tying the floors together and connecting them to the courtyard.

Via this green wall, and courtesy of a planter box, foliage spills into the master en suite on the top level of the three-storey front block. Below, from the balcony belonging to one of the children's bedrooms, the leopard tree in the courtyard seems almost within reach.

A slatted timber screen partially encloses the courtyard-facing rooms, providing shade and airflow – both crucial in tropical architecture. Privacy was also a factor. 'The original plan was to be totally connected to the courtyard and not to have the timber

A vertical garden connects the courtyard with the bedrooms on the upper floors of the main building.

The slatted screening
of a balcony attached to
a bedroom lends privacy
while affording views of
the courtyard.

screen, but our clients really liked the peekaboo effect,' says Arango. 'Also, the kitchen is very open and people always end up gathering there. They didn't want their daughter's room or the master bathroom to be clearly visible from that area.'

As with other shophouses redesigned for modern lifestyles, this project required back-and-forth consultations with the authorities, owing in part to its location within the Blair Plain conservation area (one of Singapore's historic residential districts), which placed the building in the highest preservation category. Directives were issued for everything from tiling to roof span and wall placement, particularly for the front building.

Despite less scrutiny of the rear areas, the original size and location of the courtyard were nevertheless determined through 'architectural archaeology' and more or less faithfully reproduced. 'We could see the columns where the courtyard would have started,' says Arango, 'and took it from there.'

Having to move across open space may not appeal to those Singaporeans who prefer closed, air-conditioned comfort but, for the owners, an awning high up provides adequate shelter. 'It does rain a lot here but we also have very nice days, and if we can allow air to flow through the house that is an achievement,' says Arango.

Sir Stamford would no doubt agree.

Left: The attic-level master suite includes a bathroom connected to the garden by a green wall.

Below and opposite, top: The spiral staircase is a focal point in this unusually long shophouse.

17 BLAIR ROAD

Right: The master bedroom occupies the entire top level of the front block.

Opposite: The upper floor of this restored shophouse projects over a pedestrian passage called the five-foot way.

Above: Before the courtyard's restoration, the building was cocooned in darkness.

SHADOW HOUSE
Samira Rathod Design Atelier

ALIBAG, INDIA, 2017

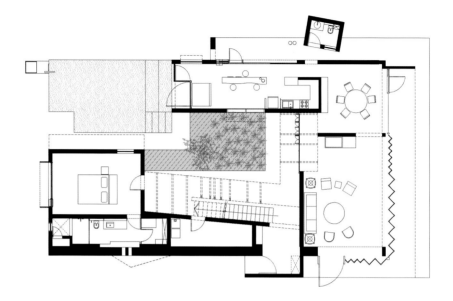

The arrival sequence for Shadow House may
have been choreographed to begin at the
compound gate, but for visitors it starts from
a greater distance and goes something like
this: spot water tower amid fields resembling
cracked earthenware; linger on scarlet
poinciana tree in the haze and bare hills over
yonder; marvel that anything so beautiful
flourishes under a summer sun that leaves
the ground baked and beaten.

Then the sound of rustling announces
a breeze and the heat spell is broken. Amid tall
waves of *Pennisetum* grasses flanking a narrow
path – alongside umbrella palms, lemongrass
and other greenery – coolness beckons.

The effect is no accident. It forms part of
a series of measures to turn the temperature
down in this 325-square-metre (3,500-sq-ft),
two-storey house in rural Alibag, a holiday
destination for India's wealthy, 120 kilometres
(75 miles) south of Mumbai. Alongside
such psychological approaches as clever
landscaping, however, are tangible strategies
for passive cooling: crucially, a courtyard at the
heart of the house.

That internal area was integral to the design
by architect Samira Rathod from the start. 'It
was a barren piece of land with sun pouring
down on it,' she says. 'My first reaction was for
it to be pampered, to be in a womb. And that
meant enclosure, so the central space became
a courtyard.'

Although a swimming pool was initially
planned for the void, cooling the house when
breezes passed over the water, Rathod's clients
opted instead for an area they could cross
easily to reach either end of the built loop.
Moved beyond the hollow, the body of water
now extends directly from wide swing doors at
the far side of the long kitchen. A low window
running almost the length of the kitchen bench
offers a direct view of the courtyard.

The 'unravelling' of the house, as Rathod
describes it, starts at, and ends in, this central
courtyard. From this spot, the house can be
unravelled again.

Immediately revealed, paradoxically, is
the dimness, aided by the overhang of
a steep corten steel roof and screening
by the buildings themselves.

Opposite: First-floor
windows, resembling
piano keys, overlook
the courtyard, which is
bordered on the ground
floor with handmade
concrete tiles.

Above: Behind the bi-fold doors is the double-height living room, to the side of which is the kitchen.

Opposite: This opening in the kitchen offers a ground-level view of the courtyard.

'This is southern Indian in the darkness and in the placement of the courtyard,' says Rathod, explaining that windows in such abodes were generally small or kept closed to ensure the sun stayed out. 'That is what we tried to create in the middle of this house; as you move out to the rooms you get your light.'

The generous use of wood (in this case recycled Burmese teak) was another southern Indian influence, especially in the bridge connecting the two en suite bedrooms upstairs. This transitional space, painted in dark hues like the rest of the house, enjoys diffused light through a phalanx of shaded windows resembling piano keys. The sense of airiness encourages pit stops en route to the bedrooms to take in the courtyard below.

'That's exactly where I expected people to sit, beer in hand,' says Rathod, catching me resting on a step. 'In the afternoon, when it gets very dark in here, streaks of light create amazing shadows.'

A separate area in which to plant yourself upstairs is an open study overlooking the lofty lounge. The ceiling heights of rooms, in addition to their sizes, reflect a hierarchy of spaces, with Rathod tending to keep bedrooms tight. 'I celebrate the idea of smallness because you take as much as you need, and leave the rest out in the open,' she says.

That includes the deep corridor of cool, pigmented concrete tiles around the courtyard. Exposed to rain – 'so you get that sense of the wetness' – the courtyard is different from

SHADOW HOUSE

Opposite: The swimming
pool extends from doors
at the far end of the
kitchen.

its counterparts in traditional southern Indian houses in one key respect. 'Normally, all the rooms open out into the courtyard,' says Rathod. In Shadow House, however, the fields and hills on the other side of the building are the focus of the living room, and none of the three bedrooms (including one on the ground floor) looks directly into the courtyard. But in moving from room to room you are constantly aware of this semi-enclosed space.

And you engage with it, which is why a babul tree – a type of *Acacia* famous for its fragrant blooms – occupies the prime spot. 'The nice thing about a courtyard is that sense of boundary,' says Rathod. 'If something is bounded you can connect with it, and when you're in that space you're in direct conversation with what is within its edges.'

Rathod continues with an explanation of the Venturi effect and how breezes in this part of the house accelerate when channelled through the relatively narrow opening between the courtyard and the pool.

Despite all these heat-relieving measures, however, we return to the ways in which our physical well-being can be affected by our imagination. 'It's also about a sense of cooling,' Rathod says, standing by the muscular concrete façade accommodating the main entrance.

Swaying grasses will do it. As will the mere suggestion of mystery. Shadow House? The name itself brings the mercury down.

Right: The corten roof
shades the courtyard.

When it eventually
blossoms, the babul
tree is expected to
scatter flowers and
scent the house.

Above: Windows on the top floor overlook the courtyard on two sides.

Right: Between the courtyard and the living room, small openings resembling wicket doors allow ventilation.

SHADOW HOUSE

Opposite page: Solid,
pigmented-concrete walls
contrast with an interior
that Samira Rathod
describes as 'crafted with
light and air'.

Below: The staircase
behind the bamboo poles
leads to a rooftop area
perfect for taking in the
surrounding landscape.

Above: Openings of different heights and shapes control the views.

Right: Porthole windows in the guest bathroom look out at tall grasses planted to give a sense of the landscape.

Opposite: The swimming pool, originally positioned in the courtyard, now laps at the kitchen doors.

RIPARIAN HOUSE
Architecture Brio

KARJAT, INDIA, 2015

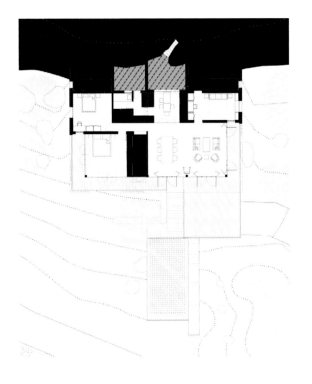

Courtyard houses as far back as antiquity have served modest home owners well in their ability to present a plain façade to the world. Riparian House went several steps further in humility. Instead of shouting out its presence high above a hillock, the building is partially buried so that, approaching it from behind, you might find yourself walking over the roof before realizing what's underfoot.

'Now we are stepping on the living room,' says architect Robert Verrijt, as we make our way across a level grassy expanse towards the river that gives the house its name. To make the most of the view, a deep wooden deck segues from the sitting area below and, lower down, the slope is terraced to accommodate a swimming pool. This simple, three-bedroom weekender, in the Western Ghats on the outskirts of Mumbai, may have fulfilled the wishes of clients attracted to the idea of a modern-day dugout, but they were initially apprehensive about the courtyards that had been included in the concept mainly for light.

'Our clients were really worried about the rain,' says Verrijt, recalling their concerns about flooding from water entering the big hole in the ground. 'We had presented a drawing that was basically the roof plan – what you would see from the top – which was a green space with a cutout and what we imagined to be a ramp going into the centre of the house.'

That roughly describes the naturally insulated, single-storey house now, although its design went through several iterations with courtyards and without. Time played a role in the to-ing and fro-ing. The first residential commission for Architecture Brio – established in 2006 by Verrijt and Shefali Balwani – took seven years to complete because of, among other things, the drawn-out application process for riverside construction. Changing circumstances during that time also required a reassessment of needs. Whereas the original brief had called for a house as compact as possible, built to a tight budget and for two people, within a few years the architects had to design a home for a family of five. The arrival of three children, and more savings in the interim, allowed the courtyards to be reinstated and the house to grow.

Opposite: The courtyard and kitchen attached to it receive the morning sun.

Pages 183–184: The living areas and master suite face the river.

However, with floor space of just 170 square metres (1,830 sq ft), Riparian House is still pocket-sized. Tucked into wide-open surroundings, with no boundary walls separating it from neighbouring properties, it also employs screens of vertical bamboo poles, beyond a steel-and-glass façade, to blend into the scenery.

'[Riparian House] is four typologies in one,' says Verrijt, adding that as much as it is a courtyard house, it is also an underground house, a veranda house and a glass house. Mullioned windows along the entire front of the building are repeated inside to separate the kitchen from its outdoor enclosure. Directly facing the river, and the mountains beyond,

are the living areas and the main, en suite bedroom, around which, on three sides of the house, is a veranda. Two other bedrooms occupy the far back corners of the house, and between them, quarried more extensively out of the ground, are the two small courtyards. Created from a 4-metre-deep (13 ft) excavation, one outdoor area, connected to a helper's room, is used for laundry. The other, separated by a rough limestone wall, is attached to the kitchen. At its extreme boundary, a set of steps, cut into the crevice between two basalt boulders, leads to the roof garden.

'The courtyard was conceived originally to allow light into the back rooms,' says Verrijt, referring to the 4 x 6-metre (13 x 20-ft) larger

Above: Beside the main courtyard is a smaller outdoor enclosure connected to a helper's room.

Opposite: Steps to the roof garden were carved from a crevice between two large rocks.

void. East facing, it captures the morning sun and admits breezes from the direction of the river. And though it looks uncannily like an ancient sinkhole, the trees on top draw your gaze towards the sky, alleviating the feeling of being buried.

Verrijt also considers this void the penultimate point along a progression that takes you from river to pool, and then up another flight of steps on the central axis to the living areas, the courtyard and, ultimately, the roof.

Clamber up to this verdant patch and you feel part of the landscape. Disappear beneath the grass, earth and concrete slab and you are part of the land. The courtyards, cut from the terrain, elevate this humble home. Their benefits do not take long to sink in.

Above: The living room is cooled by the planted roof above it.

Opposite: The progression of spaces begins at the river, from where you climb up to the pool, house and roof.

RIPARIAN HOUSE

Riparian House took seven years to complete, partly because of its riverside location.

CHAMELEON HOUSE
Word of Mouth

BALI, INDONESIA, 2017

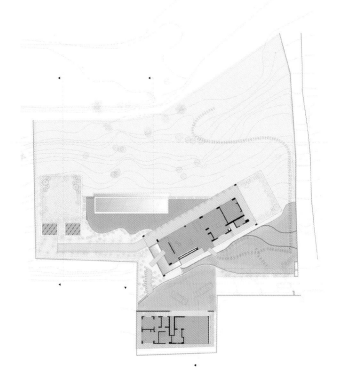

When is a courtyard house really a house
with courtyards?

You might ask this of Chameleon House,
which has two small courtyards, double that
number, or even more, depending on whose
criteria determine classification. Not that it's the
number of these outdoor areas that raises the
question, but it stands to reason that before
deciding what makes a courtyard house, one
should ask: what is a courtyard?

Examples that do and do not fit the mould
precisely can be found in the portfolio of Bali-,
Singapore- and London-based Italian-Greek
architect Valentina Audrito, of Word of Mouth.
Several of her residential designs have 'more
evident' courtyards, she says. Others need to
be experienced in person.

At Lalaland, a pre-existing home on Bali's
south coast that Audrito renovated and
landscaped for her own family, the planted
area beyond the parking zone might be judged
a front garden. But to her it is a courtyard
because of the enclosure and intimacy created
by lush planting and large sculptures within the
open arms of her L-shaped house.

It is no mere front yard, she adds, because
rooms look out into this whimsical space, walled
off from the public so it benefits the home owner
more than the neighbours (or future suburban
streetscape, given Bali's building boom).

In explaining courtyards, however, Audrito
points to different forms that have influenced
her, from West and East: the Italian cortile, for
example, is the roofless, arcaded internal court
contained within a structure. 'It's the idea of the
smaller square, where kids play,' she says. 'In
Torino, where I grew up, most kids would spend
their afternoons in the cortile because almost
every old building has one.'

Also bounded by architecture are traditional
Balinese courtyards, although these are created
by pavilions laid out around open space – a
metaphorical navel – and according to divine
cardinal directions.

In the case of Chameleon House, which
stands on a steep, jungly slope leading to
a river, Audrito adapted courtyard concepts
for her clients, also expatriates in Bali. As
with Architecture Brio's Riparian House (see
pages 180–189) in India, the objective behind

Opposite: Both river-
facing guest suites, in
a discrete block carved
out of a steep slope, have
excavated courtyards
connected to bathrooms
at the back.

Chameleon House was to allow the structure to disappear into its environment (hence the name). Rooftop planting camouflages what lies beneath – a 620-square-metre (6,670-sq-ft), linear, two-storey house whose rooms overlook the high-octane river. Two en suite bedrooms are on the bottom, as is a grotto-like chill-out zone with an outdoor kitchen beside the pool. Living areas are on the entrance level, above.

Audrito counts as two of the courtyards at Chameleon House a circumscribed area between a separate, 175-square-metre (1,885-sq-ft) staff/office building and the main pavilion, and another between this main building and a discrete guest unit. 'In a tropical country ... green filters act often as proper barriers,' she says. 'Given the contours of the land, the courtyards (or in-between spaces) are carved at different levels, offering enclaves that feel private and protected.'

Such enclaves include a triangular area conceived as a continuation of the courtyard between the main building and staff quarters.

Beneath the roof garden are the living areas and entrance. The bedrooms are on the pool level.

This 'breathing space' behind the kitchen accommodates a house temple, where offerings are made.

Two other courtyards, however, are entirely different again. In the partly subterranean, 220-square-metre (2,370-sq-ft) guest block, two river-facing bedrooms are attached to excavated bathroom courtyards that appear as square indentations from above. Down below, when all the doors in the suites are slid open to create two long rooms, the excavated chambers resemble deep stages. In addition to this element of theatre, the courtyards contribute light and air without sacrificing privacy. In the wet rooms themselves, the courtyards make special the everyday act of ablution: you feel like you're bathing outdoors.

So what is a courtyard? 'The idea is based on an open-air space defined by boundaries, and these boundaries can be walls, screens or vegetation,' Audrito offers. Notions about them, like the courtyard house itself, shape themselves according to place and plot

The top-floor deck, which runs the length of the house, overlooks a river at the bottom of the steep plot. The guest suites are beneath the lawn at the far end.

Above: Rooftop greenery allows Chameleon House to blend in with its environment, hence its name.

Right: The foyer steps down into an open living and dining area.

Right: Volcanic stone graces the poolside 'grotto'.

Below: A bridge takes you across a pond to the foyer.

Pages 196–197: Vegetation and the site's contours enclose a courtyard at the back of the house.

CHAMELEON HOUSE

Opposite page: The void at the back of the en suite bathroom adds an outdoor element to daily ablutions. Greenery cascades down the walls of the excavated courtyards.

Right: In a separate building, the light draws you down the steps towards guest rooms on either side of a 'tunnel'.

Left: This curved bathroom, by the pool, disappears into the landscape and is naturally ventilated from above.

Opposite: The en suite master bathroom relies on a wall of bamboo for privacy.

CHAMELEON HOUSE

SAIGON HOUSE
a21 studio

HO CHI MINH CITY, VIETNAM, 2015

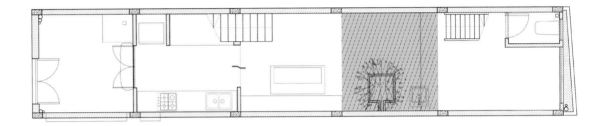

When it comes to winning approval for their designs, a21 studio are not above being underhand.

In conceptualizing a new build for a tight plot in one of Ho Chi Minh City's lively, but fast-disappearing, alleyways, they were guided by their client's request for a traditional Saigon house, evoking the city of yesteryear. But when it came to garnering support for their ideas, they went straight to young family members who would one day bring up their own children in the building.

'When we were designing the house and making a model for it we didn't present it to the parents; we showed it to the kids,' says architect Toan Nghiem about the white-brick house, built, where possible, with salvaged materials, including tiles and wood. 'If the kids liked it, we knew their parents, even if they didn't feel comfortable about it, would follow.'

The studio's fun, nostalgic design, however, appealed across the generations. The grown-ups – who expressly eschewed a Western-style glass-and-steel structure, like many of the new buildings sprouting up around the city – warmed to a21 studio's suggestion of an internal courtyard amid rooms made to look like small, colourful houses facing each other across an alley.

And the children enjoyed the quirkiness of a house with small rooms perfectly suited to hide-and-seek. Best of all was a playground created with them in mind: strung above the courtyard is heavy-duty mesh resembling a circus safety net. Connecting the front and rear of the house, this perforated surface provides the children with an open-air games area away from, but in sight of, the adults hanging out below.

Like many of Vietnam's narrow but deep houses, Saigon House is wedged into a skinny plot, measuring only 3 x 15 metres (10 x 50 ft) – a legacy of old property taxes calculated on the street-front widths of buildings. Above its green wooden front door an intricate steel veil covers its face and extends over the top of the building. The 135-square-metre (1,455-sq-ft) structure, open above the 3 x 5-metre (10 x 16-ft) courtyard, is intended one day to support a leafy tapestry that filters air, noise and light.

Opposite: The courtyard, with its star fruit tree, separates the front and back sections of this narrow house.

Above: The owners
wanted to recreate the
feel of an old Saigon alley.

Opposite and right: Green
wooden doors lead into
a twenty-first-century
alley house, with steel
latticework on the upper
floors providing security
and doubling as a trellis
for creeping plants.

Opposite: Roofs over individual rooms, painted in bright colours, give them the appearance of miniature houses.

Adding to the greenness is the star fruit tree in the courtyard, where the family gathers in fine weather for communal meals. This central open space divides the three-storey rear block from the front end, which climbs an additional level and is distinguished, in section, by sloped roofs for each of five rooms. Those facing the courtyard can be shuttered for privacy or have their windows flung open for air and light. The theatricality is enhanced by a Juliet balcony extending from the top bedroom, which looks down, through tree branches and the play net, to the courtyard.

Separate series of staircases connect the levels on both sides: turn back on yourself in the kitchen on the ground floor and you climb up into the family zone; proceed across the concrete courtyard, under an umbrella if it's raining, and it's likely you're a visitor renting the back quarters.

When the family alone inhabits the house, the courtyard serves as a channel for direct communication. Having grown up in a house with only one set of stairs connecting its levels, Nghiem remembers the challenges of interaction between the floors (his mother resorting to phoning him down for dinner). 'But in Saigon House, it's easy,' he says. 'If you're on the ground floor, you just shout up to someone in a room above.'

Despite Saigon House depending on the courtyard for amenity, Nghiem contends that its design did not begin with the internal void, and that function rather than form defines the space. As with the romantic recreation of the feeling of an ancient alleyway, he uses sensations to describe its existence: 'We consider the courtyard to be the movement of air.'

Right: Strung over the courtyard is a net on which the children play.

207

Opposite: An open workroom occupies the first level of the front block.

Right: A sitting room in the duplex in the back block has an immediate view of the courtyard tree.

Below: Plants are to be enticed up the steel veil.

3 HOUSES
AD+studio

HO CHI MINH CITY, VIETNAM, 2016

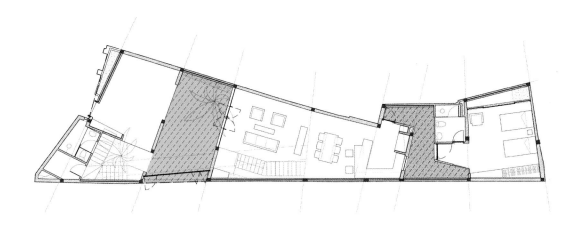

'Ugly.' That's how the owner of 3 Houses describes the land on which his new home stands. Not only is the plot long and skinny – par for the course in Ho Chi Minh City – but it is also zigzagged and landlocked: buildings of varying heights hem in the plot, corseting it at the waist.

But instead of going higher for relief, following the neighbourhood trend, Dung Nguyen, of AD+studio, kept things relatively low (for Vietnam) and went with the flow. Recognizing the need for security in addition to the usual air, light and privacy, the architect came up with 3 Houses: a trio of discrete two- and three-storey blocks separated from each other by a couple of courtyards, and linked via bridges and a folded roof.

'3 Houses exploits the site and at the same time reveals its shortcomings through its shape,' says Nguyen, who studied architecture in Vietnam but says he designed the residence without specific cultural references to his country. White and angular, the structure is also distinctive because of its triangular-faceted, origami-like roof and use of louvres, which

extend from the top of the structure down its façade.

Each of the three blocks on the 175-square-metre (1,880-sq-ft) plot plays a different role, with private quarters and work areas at either end, and a space for everyone in the middle. Here, the living room enjoys a double-height ceiling that achieves maximum drama with light slicing through the concrete louvres.

Illumination enters not only from above but also through two openings to courtyards: an interior picture window revealing a small exterior space and, at the other end, soaring glass panels giving on to the main outdoor area.

Flanked by the office and middle blocks, this 24-square-metre (258-sq-ft) courtyard is further bounded by a tall brick wall and imposing gates that close off the 150-square-metre (1,610-sq-ft) house at the end of a street. Apart from being used as a foyer, it doubles as a safe playground for the owner's young child, and somewhere to park a motorcycle or three (only a tiny percentage of households in Vietnam have cars).

Opposite: 3 Houses comprises three blocks of different heights, separated by courtyards and connected by bridges.

As with many subtropical homes, the main courtyard in 3 Houses employs simple passive design strategies to minimize energy use inside. High walls provide shade and reduce radiant heat, and, in future, a latticework of creepers overhead will act as an evergreen filter. These basic climate-control measures allow air conditioning to be limited mostly to the property's three bedrooms.

Energy savings alone, however, often fail to sway opinion about the cost-worthiness of courtyards. 'They are not popular in Ho Chi Minh City because land is so expensive,' says Nguyen. 'People here try to make use of the whole plot.'

But good ventilation being one of the client's demands, two courtyards were positioned opposite each other for optimum effect. Such a layout mirrors the alternate mass–void compositions that aid airflow in shophouses and tube houses: the deeper the structures, the more such openings. In contrast to the 100-metre-long (328 ft) structures that were

built in Hanoi's Old Quarter, 3 Houses is 30 metres (98 ft) from nose to tail and 3.7 metres (12 ft) at its narrowest point.

At half the size of the main courtyard, the second void is better characterized as a 'sky yard'. It acts as a buffer between public and private spaces and, as with Saigon House (see pages 202–209), aids communication between the floors. Partially open to the elements, and full of plants where rain falls, this internal outdoor space also provides evaporative cooling and, positioned in front of the kitchen sink, is a distraction from dishwashing drudgery.

Although both outdoor areas are visible from within the main block, they are perhaps best appreciated from the top of the office wing. From here the louvres over the minor courtyard resemble fish gills and the folded roof effectively transitions between the tall and the short. Constrained though the 'ugly' plot may be, the house to which it gave rise is a breath of fresh air.

Louvres connected to folded roofs snake through the landlocked site.

The larger of two entrances, off a 5-metre-wide (16 ft) lane, takes you directly into the main courtyard.

Above, left and right:
The angular concrete
ceiling of the double-
height living room
is a reminder of the
zigzagging plot.

Opposite: Natural light
enters the main building
through overhead louvres
and the glass curtain wall
by the main courtyard.

Left and below: The kitchen at the back of the middle block looks into a 'sky yard', which can also be seen from the bridge to the family room a level above.

Opposite: The main courtyard made it possible to inhabit the hemmed-in plot.

3 HOUSES

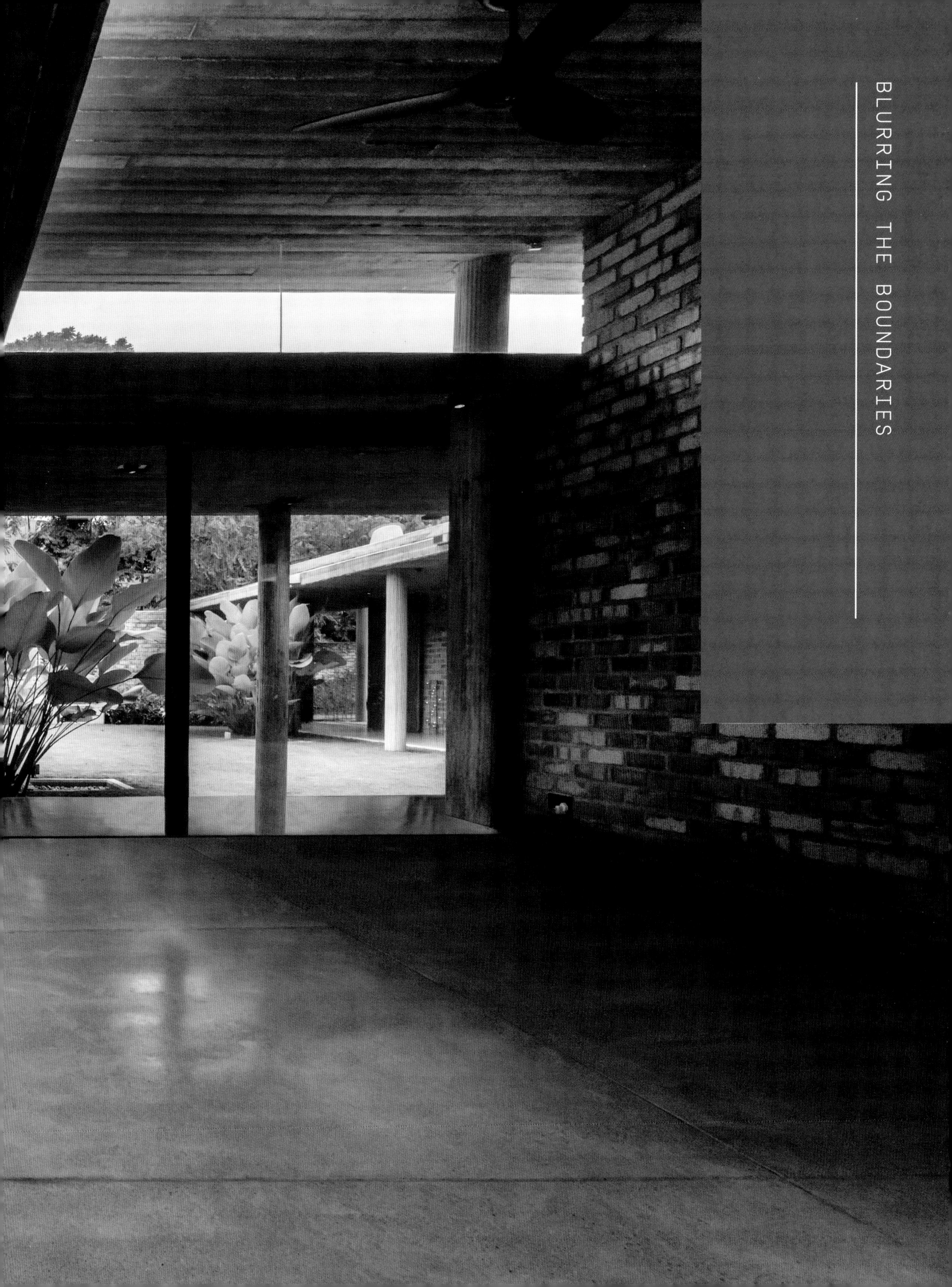

BLURRING THE BOUNDARIES

'Inviting the outdoors in' has become something of a design cliché, but in these houses the phrase takes on special meaning because living areas are open to the elements day and night. Blinds can be deployed at Suryamzhu, and were supposed to have been installed at Umah Tampih – before its owners decided they preferred total exposure – but the most important rooms in these courtyard houses are intended to be enjoyed without walls interrupting the flow. At Gomati House, sliding glass panels can close off the courtyard-level family room, but the extensive transition areas, which are open, ensure the entire floor feels like a jungle, manicured in the middle for human habitation. Taking the outside-in concept to its extreme is the studio home created for two Sri Lankan artists who wanted to minimize costs and maximize air circulation. Doing without walls on two, sometimes three sides of their rooms achieves just that.

SURYAMZHU
Design Unit

PETALING JAYA, MALAYSIA, 2017

Engage Malaysians on the topic of weather and you're likely to hear such grumbles as: 'There are ten suns out there.' Or this, from my aunt, who says of her home in the capital: 'Kuala Lumpur's either hot and humid, or hot, wet and even more humid.'

'KL'-based British architect John Bulcock, however, brightens at the mention of his adoptive country's equatorial climate. Known for his passive-building designs in the region, Thailand and Sri Lanka included, the founder of Design Unit speaks not of the shortcomings associated with high temperatures and mugginess, but of how to take advantage of the 'fantastic climate' and site conditions to create homes that can be comfortable without requiring much auxiliary support.

In neighbouring Petaling Jaya, a client cleaved to that approach for a new build she wanted to be a 'canvas' for creativity. Her brief, which also stipulated simplicity and a garden 'very much a part of the house', led to a single-storey, three-bedroom home with a 97-square-metre (1,040-sq-ft) central courtyard that helps cool, ventilate and light the rooms naturally.

Apart from reducing building energy requirements, the courtyard at Suryamzhu (which means 'sun ray') is important in other ways as well. Wanting the house to adhere to basic Vastu Shastra principles, its owner welcomed the creation of a garden in the middle, which, according to the Hindu science of architecture, allows an unobstructed flow of positive energy (feng shui shares similar ideals). Like many other Vastu-compliant homes, rooms are arranged around the courtyard, believed to be the most powerful zone in the house.

Vastu also guided the positioning of the unadorned main entrance, which, auspiciously, faces northeast (tapping the rising sun's vital energy). But you'd be forgiven for overlooking its significance because of the unanticipated beauty that awaits you just within.

Turn a corner by the perforated, fair-faced brick wall beside the driveway – a privacy barrier blocking views from the street but allowing breezes through – and you mentally cross a threshold into a world unto itself. 'I like

Pages 218–219: At Suryamzhu, the courtyard is an extension of the main rooms, including the bedroom closest to the living areas.

Opposite: Blinds can be deployed when it rains but otherwise the living areas remain open, maximizing natural light and ventilation.

SURYAMZHU

An open-sided walkway
borders the courtyard
and links the rooms.

this surprising space when you walk in,' says Bulcock. 'You don't know what to expect.'

Across a patch of turf, a see-through concrete-and-glass pavilion, designed to 'hover' over a reflective pond, affords views of neighbouring trees. Taking you there is a walkway hugging the courtyard and connecting the main rooms: clockwise, a kitchen-and-casual-dining area; guest accommodation, with its own entrance; a large en suite bedroom; and the living-room pavilion, the destination.

It is in this main pavilion that the effect of indoor–outdoor living is immediately obvious. In the middle section, a casual bar and sitting area relies on blinds rather than solid walls to keep out the rain. Otherwise, it is open to a view of trees on one side and, on the other, the courtyard.

Flanking this breezy lounge are glass boxes that contain formal living and dining rooms at either end. But fold back their doors and these areas also become open-air spaces that spill out on to an external, cantilevered deck spanning the site. Beneath it, a 14-metre (46-ft) swimming pool makes use of a previously overgrown strip at the bottom of a slope.

Like many suburban homes, the original house had faced the road and occupied the middle of the plot (a typical sight in suburbs, where gardens often become dead spaces unused at the front owing to a lack of privacy, and neglected at the back). Turning the new building around closed it to public scrutiny – a boon in security-conscious Malaysia – and enabled it to create its own context. But instead of focusing the gaze solely inwards, the way many courtyard houses do, Suryamzhu

The main building was designed to 'float' above a reflective pond.

also looks out, through the glass pavilion, enhancing the sense of space and capitalizing on the natural setting beyond.

Of course, planting a courtyard in the centre also added flexibility. 'The idea was that you could always have the outdoors set up for dinner, giving you easy access to the kitchen,' says the owner. 'It's quite cool at night; I just have to put up citronella sticks for mosquitoes.'

Like the other versatile public rooms, the kitchen can be opened on opposite sides, obviating the need for a separate, outdoor kitchen for pungent cooking (a favoured setup in many Malaysian homes).

All of which makes sense of Bulcock's take on not only passive design but also sustainability, which he insists is not merely about materials and their impact on nature.

'It's actually about the psychological effect of the house,' he says. 'It could be totally self-sufficient in terms of energy consumption, but if it's not a joy to use, to me it's not sustainable.'

Step into this house and you'll understand the advantage of ten suns.

Precast concrete slabs were used on the roof terrace.

A deck the width of the site cantilevers towards the swimming pool, which was built into what had previously been an unused slope.

ARC HOUSE

Kevin O'Brien Architects

BRISBANE, AUSTRALIA, 2016

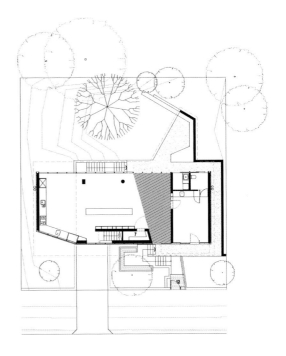

Architects' own homes are often laboratories brimming with ideas and experiments seeking validation. Kevin O'Brien's hillcrest house in Brisbane, Australia, fits both descriptions, although academic influence and heritage also determined its materiality and design. Finding expression in the house he shares with his wife, fellow architect Susan Ellison, and their two children, are aspects of her Irish background and his Torres Strait Islander ancestry.

Destined to be a courtyard house from the start, their family home, says O'Brien, was always conceived with a void open to the elements. 'I was just trying to figure out, "What if you make a hole [in the house], what else can it do?"'

By reinterpreting the archetypal form of the courtyard house, O'Brien came up with a two-storey trapezoidal space that conceptually enables introversion while fostering interconnection. Practically speaking, however, the court draws in light and promotes ventilation.

ARC House, which eschews glass, is illuminated naturally through translucent polycarbonate panels and clear acrylic windows and doors. The beauty of the PC panels is most obvious on the top floor, where three bedrooms that pinwheel around the void are bathed in a gentle, diffused light. Downstairs, the more public living areas open on to the courtyard.

The rectangular house – inhabiting the 20 x 20-metre (65 x 65-ft) backyard of a subdivided plot – benefits from the courtyard in other ways. Being overlooked by several properties in proximity, it boasts a private zone that bares itself to few: the bedrooms are cloistered, their gaze turned inwards towards the courtyard deck.

'Even though there are views to the city [from the house], we've shut them down,' says O'Brien. 'The only thing I really want to know about is that mountain range over there.'

A view of Mount Coot-tha determined the siting of the outdoor dining area, just beyond the courtyard. Gatherings thus have a connection to this landmark, an Aboriginal ancestral entity whose name refers to the area's native bee. 'It is Mecca-like; sometimes

Opposite: The courtyard separates the living areas from a guest apartment. A floor above, bedroom windows open into the void.

ARC HOUSE

you can't see it, but you know where it is and where you are relative to it,' adds O'Brien.

In a broader context, ARC House offers that feeling of relief through being able to locate yourself indoors or out. Apart from allowing a direct link to the sky from 'inside', the opening allows you, before stepping outdoors, to 'feel the humidity and smell whatever's flowering'.

Memories of the years he spent in Ireland as a young architect prompt O'Brien to observe that, in cold climates, a fireplace, rather than a courtyard, might be the point in a home around which life revolves. 'Here we have air in the centre,' he says. 'The thing I hated when I lived in Dublin was being trapped inside a box.'

There is little risk of claustrophobia in ARC House, where the element of air integral to its design is apparent the minute you step

through the entrance. A covered breezeway leads to the courtyard, where compression finds release as you emerge into the open.

Physically, the space separates a self-contained studio from the open-plan living areas: a kitchen, which looks out on to the street; and dining and lounge areas, which engage with a garden on the other side. Interestingly, no fence exists outside to separate the house from a neighbouring property, so land (and a dog) can be shared. The lack of boundaries explains why O'Brien talks of a reasonably open-door policy for neighbours and family in the public zone.

Materials on this level and elsewhere were kept simple, limited to little more than concrete and spotted gum. Concrete 'wet trades' point to his wife's Irish heritage, says O'Brien, while

Indigenous Australian
artist Fiona Foley created
the bodhi leaves adorning
a wall in the courtyard.

Below: Outside the courtyard, the sitting-out area was positioned to face Mount Coot-tha, an Aboriginal ancestral entity.

Pages 236–237: On the upper level, translucent polycarbonate panels soften the light entering the bedrooms, which can breathe because of openings into the courtyard.

wood used for light-framed structures and cladding reflects a regional attitude to building.

Although O'Brien and his family moved into their home in 2011, before completion, the seeds for ARC House were planted years earlier, when he was a student at the University of Queensland. His mentor there, Professor Peter O'Gorman, showed him why courtyards provided the correct settings for life. That conviction took root with the celebrated multi-courtyard Mooloomba House, designed by Andresen O'Gorman Architects, which O'Brien helped to build in the 1990s on North Stradbroke Island, near Brisbane.

Two decades later, the interaction and introspection that courtyard houses encourage are his to call home.

ARC HOUSE

ARTISTS' STUDIO
Palinda Kannangara Architects

COLOMBO, SRI LANKA, 2017

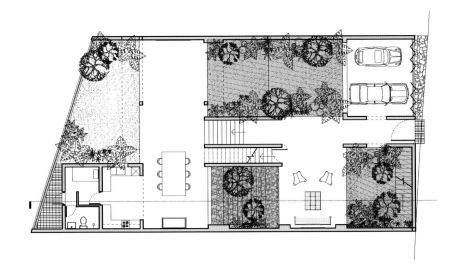

'In Sri Lanka, the vernacular is still a living tradition.' That observation, made twenty years ago in the authoritative tome *The Architecture of an Island*, may remain true today, but architects are also devising twenty-first-century updates.

Palinda Kannangara is among them. A 'third generation' architect since Geoffrey Bawa put Sri Lanka on the modernist map, Kannangara incorporates tried-and-tested strategies for tropical living in contemporary homes that satisfy the continuing desire, even among urban dwellers, to co-exist with nature. For one client, an up-and-coming artist, he designed a low-budget family home, studio and future gallery all in one.

A series of courtyards made that possible for J. C. Ratnayake, the hands-on client of Kannangara who had acquired an empty site near the Southern Expressway on the outskirts of Colombo. He would self-manage the pro bono project, and partly self-build (for three years) to save on cost.

In the split-level 'spinal' house Kannangara designed for the sloping 340-square-metre (3,660-sq-ft) plot, his 'architecture supports landscape' ethos draws on a personal preference for living spaces flanked by gardens and courtyards.

Exterior brick walls are perforated on the upper level for airflow (no air conditioners are to be found in the house). The 330-square-metre (3,552-sq-ft) dwelling – with half as much space again in internal gardens – features courtyards on both sides of the backbone, turning part of the floor plan into what, from a bird's-eye view, resembles a chequerboard of grey and green.

The building's linear arrangement may explain why it is also described as a house with courtyards as opposed to a courtyard house – especially when compared to the traditional Sri Lankan typology, in which the courtyard is central and ringed by rooms. (In other setups to be found in the island nation, rooms are clustered around smaller courtyards and screened by walls.)[1]

According to veteran architect C. Anjalendran, who has designed celebrated courtyard houses in the country, courtyard

Opposite: The house was designed with no windows, in part to lower building costs.

238

design is now based on 'pleasure'. The traditional courtyard was a utilitarian space, he says, although 'each culture – the Sinhalese, Tamils, Muslims, Dutch – used [it] differently'. Colonial influence also saw the introduction of verandas and 'divided space for "foreign" masters and "indigenous" servants'.[2]

At Ratnayake's house, which he shares with his printmaker wife, Thanuja, the upper and lower levels delineate private and public. Three bedrooms and a family room occupy the top floor, while the studio takes up half of a huge volume on the lowest level. Completely open on opposite sides to greenery – including clumps of air-purifying elephant-ear plants and other natives harvested from neighbouring plots – it is a naturally lit workspace that allows paint and other fumes to dissipate quickly.

The room is also welcoming: an open kitchen and a salvaged baker's workbench (now a dining table) share the studio floor. This area merges into an outdoor space;

but instead of mirroring the studio with its planted courtyard, it takes the form of wide stone steps. These provide casual access to a sitting room on the entrance level above and afford ample seating for art talks and other gatherings.

All of which highlights that, notwithstanding a small budget (US$65,000) and a one-year hiatus to build up funds, Ratnayake achieved his goal of creating a relaxing, nature-filled environment in which to live, work and entertain.

Apart from the usual advantages of courtyards – ventilation, light, privacy, beauty – those inserted into the layout of Ratnayake's house minimized outlay. Having indoor areas flow directly into the gardens saved on additional exterior wall surfaces, which increase the cost of many courtyard houses.

No glass is used anywhere on the ground level, meaning all rooms enjoy full cross ventilation – 'a must in Sri Lanka', as Kannangara says. But the house is not

Beside the main entrance are bi-fold doors that hide a garage.

ARTISTS' STUDIO

completely weatherproof, he acknowledges, explaining the difficulty in keeping the floor dry during heavy rain. The inconvenience earns a shrug from the homeowner. 'We wipe everything down and it's fine,' Ratnayake says. Mosquitoes and other insects have not bothered the family either, he adds, and snakes have difficulty moving across the slippery, polished cut-cement floor.

So determined are Ratnayake and his wife to live in the grip of nature that their bedroom is also open to the greenery below. A bench to the side of the suite provides a meditative spot. Directly facing a pond built above the garage roof, it brings to mind Bawa's belief that 'architecture cannot be totally explained but must be experienced'.

The courtyards in Ratnayake's home studio are essential to that experience.

The sitting room steps down to a dining area and kitchen.

ARTISTS' STUDIO

Opposite, left and top right: Concrete, recycled timber and exposed brickwork feature throughout the house.

Opposite, bottom: A courtyard flows from the studio, which shares the lowest floor with the dining area and kitchen.

Right: J. C. Ratnayake's artwork is dotted around the house, as seen here on the private, top floor.

ARTISTS' STUDIO

Opposite page: Walls
surfaced with ochre-
coloured plaster warm
the bedrooms and living
room upstairs.

Above: Beside the main
bedroom is a sitting area
that takes in the pond on
the garage roof.

GOMATI HOUSE
SPASM Design Architects

MALAVLI, INDIA, 2016

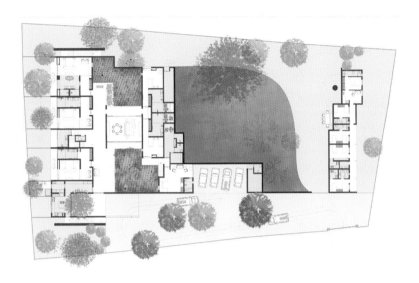

Clambering all over someone's home is not generally advisable, but at Gomati House it is a lovely way to reach the living areas on the top floor.

The climb, which begins from a curved path beneath shady trees, proceeds up a knoll, continues past a long swimming pool and ends about 4.5 metres (15 ft) above the driveway. Look up and you see a sleek, glazed pavilion; over its roof, and there are the Malavli hills, to which Mumbaiites gravitate during summer; back down, and you are in a tropical grove.

So verdant is the view from this vantage point that it is hard to imagine it any other way. But if the trees could speak, they would tell of a time when they were an afterthought. Then, the house occupying this 3,700-square-metre (39,830-sq-ft) plot had tried without success to capitalize on the mountain vistas alone. Worse, it had failed structurally, which is why, after years of fearing a collapse, the owners decided to demolish the twenty-year-old building and start afresh.

'You're actually walking over the old house,' says SPASM Design Architects' Sanjeev Panjabi

as we make the gentle ascent over grass. Rubble – including the original roof – was used to create a one-and-a-half-storey mound that became part of the new 975-square-metre (10,495-sq-ft) home. For this, Panjabi and his wife, studio co-founder Sangeeta Merchant, gave their clients simple, straight lines and a 'wallpaper' of green. 'We turned the house the other way,' says Panjabi. 'The dumbness of the original house was that it didn't look at the trees.'

With the project's raison d'être being the protection of the fifty-plus mature species on site, creating courtyards that would make way for them was a given. 'Weaving a house around trees is a sensible way to bring inside and outside into close connection,' says Panjabi. 'And apart from the obvious gains, a patch of sky is the most beautiful thing to have inside your home. It allows you to sense the passage of time.'

In summer, the upper level of Gomati House enjoys not only yellow-topped laburnums and red poincianas at the bottom of the knoll, but also the luxuriant trees growing in the

Opposite: Courtyard greenery links the two levels of the house, with the fruit from mango trees within arm's reach from the top floor.

GOMATI HOUSE

Opposite, top: Rubble from the old house lies beneath the mound.

Opposite, bottom: The primary objective was to protect the trees already growing on the site.

Pages 250–251: Stereophonic birdsong adds to the ambience of the family room.

courtyards below. Palm fronds and branches laden with mangoes poke through two large cutouts on the expansive terrace, which extends from a living room and dining area flanked and divided by staircases.

If the breezes upstairs carry away the sounds of wildlife, downstairs the chirrups, squawks and birdsong seem magnified. The stereophonic effect is particularly evident in the family room, which sits between the pair of courtyards and can be opened on two sides to the elements. In wet weather discreet rain chains help guide water runoff, and during heavy downpours blinds can be anchored around the courtyards to keep the interior surfaces dry.

Even without the rain, however, this bottom floor, partially sunken into the mound, offers respite. Its lushly planted courtyards reduce indoor air temperature through evaporative cooling.

Giant monsteras and philodendrons added to the existing trees also help to filter the light, enhancing the grey-blues of the textured stone floors throughout. 'The whole house is an expression in one stone,' says Panjabi, referring to kota (a type of limestone, quarried in Rajasthan), chosen because of its texture and hue.

The same material clads the walls, including the monolithic barrier – promising immovability – alongside the driveway. On the bottom floor, kota also appears in the kitchen (which has its own courtyard) and the five bedrooms, designed to be introverted refuges around the existing trees. This being a holiday home, two rooms are for guests; the remainder, on the opposite side, are for members of the extended family (Gomati is the name of the owner's mother).

The dissimilarity between the two levels of the house is not lost on Panjabi, who describes the bright upper pavilion as the antithesis of the lower storey. 'It's a reversal,' he says, pointing out the big-sky openness of one in contrast to the cosiness of the other.

Greenery, nevertheless, connects the two levels and affords the top floor priceless views that had been rejected before. 'The trees are the protagonists,' says Panjabi. 'We built a story around them.'

Above: The dining room, at one end of the top floor, is separated from the living area by a set of stairs.

Opposite, top: The living room extends on to a terrace with views of the courtyards below and the garden and swimming pool beyond.

Opposite, bottom: The bedrooms on the lower floor are attached to private outdoor areas.

GOMATI HOUSE

UMAH TAMPIH
Area Designs

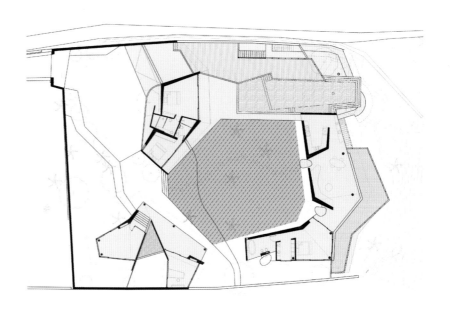

A courtyard is often referred to as the heart of a house, but in Bali the courtyard is thought of as the navel. On this Indonesian island of the gods – where residential compounds are believed to accommodate the sacred and profane, reflected in body from head to tail – these *natah* lie at the centre of activity and, by extension, communal-living ideals. In fact, so much are these outdoor spaces a part of society that the late, great landscape designer Made Wijaya described Balinese architecture as an architecture of courtyards.

Umah Tampih is a unique, twenty-first-century expression of this building convention. Comprising three discrete buildings positioned around a circular courtyard in the middle of a square-ish plot, the Ubud home of a New York couple is sensitive to the fundamental building precepts observed throughout the centuries by the island's Hindu-animist people.

Key among these precepts is spatial order, achieved in part through orientation. Even in modern suburbia, as Wijaya noted in his classic tome, *Architecture of Bali*, basic alignments are respected – house temple (or head) in the

northeast, kitchen in the south, and so on – to establish harmony with the universe. In concrete terms, for those uncomfortable with the ineffable, Umah Tampih feels as good as it looks.

'[Cheong Yew Kuan, of Area Designs] often talked about the flow of energy and space during the design process,' says photographer Jan Tyniec, who with his wife, designer Christyne Forti, gave the celebrated Malaysian-born, Bali-based architect only basic guidelines in determining what would suit them and their land, which extends down from a ridge overlooking the Ayung River Valley.

'We were drawn to vernacular materials and local tradition, and hoped they could be incorporated into the building in a modern way,' says Forti. 'Cheong proposed a ribbon flowing through space, an origami concept regarding roof shape and unity between buildings.'

In addition to experimenting with folded concrete planes that form the roofscape, walls and floor (*tampih* refers to the folds; *umah* means 'house'), Cheong divined a mandala-

Opposite, top: Indoor and outdoor spaces at Umah Tampih were given equal attention.

Opposite, bottom: The guest house is one of three buildings around the courtyard.

Above: In front of the guest house, the infinity pool cantilevers over the ridge.

Left: An intimate outdoor nook divides the split-level studio into two work areas.

Right: From the main building the kitchen enjoys full-frontal views of the valley.

Below: The living room gives new meaning to 'open plan'.

Above: At Umah Tampih, says Jan Tyniec, 'No walls meet at right angles; no walls are precisely perpendicular to floors. They tilt and slant ever so slightly.'

Above, right: Brick walls,
including those in the
guest house, feature
patterned perforations.

like courtyard, positioned to pull you through the compound and into the main building. Forti likens this largely open-sided structure, housing a kitchen, lounge and master bedroom, to a 'gate' that dramatically unlocks and frames glorious views of the valley and seven silhouetted mountains beyond.

The other two buildings consist of a guesthouse and a split-level shared studio with its own intimate courtyard accommodating a fish pond. On the upper floor, Forti's space is the larger of the two work areas and enjoys oblique views of the main house shrine. Its position, determined by a priest, faces Mount Agung, the island's highest and holiest peak.

From the beginning, Cheong had determined that indoor and outdoor spaces should be accorded equal importance, and that the central courtyard would serve different roles, including creating a link and allowing a separation of functions.

'The courtyard is also used every day for offerings,' says Forti, adding that at special events it comes into its own when gamelan musicians and *legong* dancers use the grassy area as an open stage.

According to Tyniec, the sound properties of the performance space enhance the magic. 'Because of all the subtle angles in the walls of the buildings there are good acoustics,' he says.

As we walk through the grounds, the 'gate' drawing us towards heavenly views, Cheong observes that traditional Balinese houses are basically walled compounds with pavilions around a central space. He notes that the archetype, full of light and air and surrounded by rooms, is common around the world, for example in Moroccan riads and the fast-disappearing quadrangle houses of Beijing.

But there is no denying that Umah Tampih is trussed tightly to Bali, and not just because it respects the cardinal directions. Like the island's old residential compounds, dotted with *bale* (thatched-roof structures without walls), this contemporary home benefits from openness and the courtyard at its core.

'There are no indoor or outdoor spaces in our house,' says Tyniec. 'There are spaces that enhance the site and incorporate the surrounding landscape – not only the land, but the spirit of it.'

UMAH TAMPIH

Opposite, top: The master
bedroom opens to
greenery on one side
and a deck in front.

Opposite, bottom: The
primary view from this
bedroom, one of two in
the guest house, is of
the courtyard.

Above: The main building,
with its angled roofline,
acts as a frame for
picturesque views.

Three buildings on the plot
bound the mandala-like
courtyard in the middle.

UMAH TAMPIH

NOTES

Introduction

1 Simon Unwin, *The Ten Most Influential Buildings in History*, Oxon: Routledge, 2017.

2 Robert Nelson, 'The Courtyard Inside and Out: A Brief History of an Architectural Ambiguity', *Enquiry* 11 (1): 8–17, 2014.

3 Maher Laffah, 'The Courtyard Garden in the Traditional Arab House' in *Courtyard Housing: Past, Present, and Future*, ed. Brian Edwards *et al.*, Oxon: Taylor & Francis, 2006.

House by the Lake

1 Julio Bermudez *et al.*, two-part lecture 'fMRI Study of Architecturally Induced Contemplative States', at the Academy of Neuroscience for Architecture 2012 and 2014 Conferences at the Salk Institute in San Diego, CA.

Artists' Studio

1 Ronald Lewcock, Barbara Sansoni, Laki Senanayake, *The Architecture of an Island*, Colombo, Barefoot, 1998.

2 Jilly Traganou and Miodrag Mitrasinovic, eds, *Travel, Space, Architecture*, Farnham, Ashgate Publishing, 2009.

FURTHER READING

Berliner, Nancy and Yin Yu Tang, *The Architecture and Daily Life of a Chinese House* (Tuttle Publishing, 2003).

Blaser, Werne, *Courtyard House in China* (Birkhäuser Basel, 1979).

Bracken, Gregory, *The Shanghai Alleyway House* (Routledge, 2013).

Edwards, Brian, et al. eds, *Courtyard Housing: Past, Present and Future* (Taylor & Francis, 2006).

Goad, Philip and Anoma Pieris, *New Directions in Tropical Asian Architecture* (Periplus, 2005).

Inglis, Kim, *Bali by Design* (Tuttle Publishing, 2012).

Isozaki, Arata, et al., *Katsura Imperial Villa* (Electa Architecture, 2005).

Knapp, Ronald and Kai-Yin Lo, eds, *House Home Family* (University of Hawaii Press, 2005).

Keister, Douglas, *Courtyards: Intimate Outdoor Spaces* (Gibbs Smith, 2005).

Knapp, Ronald G., *China's Vernacular Architecture* (University of Hawaii Press, 1989).

Knapp, Ronald G., *Chinese Houses* (Tuttle Publishing, 2005).

Lewcock, Ronald, Barbara Sansoni and Laki Senanayake, *The Architecture of an Island* (Barefoot, 1998).

Lin, Lee Loh-lim, *The Blue Mansion* (L'Plan, 2002).

McCartney, Karen, *50/60/70: Iconic Australian Houses* (Murdoch Books, 2007).

McGillick, Paul, *The Sustainable Asian House* (Tuttle Publishing, 2013).

McGillick, Paul, *Sustainable Luxury* (Tuttle Publishing, 2015).

Macintosh, Duncan, *The Modern Courtyard House* (Architectural Association Papers, 1973).

Pfeifer, Günter and Per Brauneck, *Courtyard Houses: A Housing Typology* (Birkhäuser Verlag, 2008).

Powell, Robert, *The Modern Thai House* (Tuttle Publishing, 2012).

Rabbat, Nasser O., *The Courtyard House* (Ashgate, 2010).

Reyes, Elizabeth V., *25 Tropical Houses in the Philippines* (Periplus, 2005).

Robson, David, *Anjalendran: Architect of Sri Lanka* (Tuttle Publishing, 2009).

Silveira, Angelo Costa, *Lived Heritage, Shared Space* (Yoda Press, 2008).

Smith, Kathryn, *Schindler House* (Hennessey + Ingalls, 2010).

Tanizaki, Junichiro, *In Praise of Shadows* (Vintage, 2001).

Unwin, Simon, *The Ten Most Influential Buildings in History* (Routledge, 2017).

Wijaya, Made, *Architecture of Bali* (University of Hawaii Press, 2002).

Zhang, Donia, *Courtyard Housing and Cultural Sustainability* (Routledge, 2016).

Zhang, Donia, *Courtyard Housing for Health and Happiness* (Routledge, 2017).

PICTURE CREDITS

All architectural plans are courtesy of the architects, with green highlights to show courtyard areas added by Thames & Hudson.

ACKNOWLEDGMENTS

Dedicated to my parents, who created an improbable Japanese garden in Malaysia.
And to my pebble-colouring brothers, who led me up the garden path with their 'precious' blue stone.

This book was made possible by the generosity of architects, photographers, home owners, friends and family. Thank you to the scores of people who spared their time and opened doors (their own and those of others). I'm indebted to the architects who accompanied me on sometimes far-flung site visits in scorching conditions (Samira Rathod, Robert Verrijt and Sanjeev Panjabi, I'm thinking of you): I'm so glad you understood why I needed to step into rooms, outdoor ones included, to write about them.

I often feel more like an anthropologist than a design writer when asking people how they live. Much obliged especially to Ranggani Puspandya, Michael and Anwen Batchelor, Tze-Chun Wei, Kevin O'Brien, Palinda Kannangara and Lisa Hochhauser for making me feel welcome in your homes.

Two giants of architecture who gave my work extra meaning were Andra Matin, five of whose projects I visited, including his own cat-friendly home, in Jakarta; and C. Anjalendran, who took me on a day trip to Mirissa, Sri Lanka, to see Mount Cinnamon, a courtyard house he designed in 2002 that remains one of my favourites. Thank you both.

My gratitude also to Ken Yeang, Marc Almagro and Ross Urwin, whose cottage in Mullumbimby allowed me to eat in and kick back, often impossible on my short, madly packed trips. And to Mark Swanton, of Ke-zu, and Dave Beeman, of Vampt Vintage Design: borrowing your beautiful kit to furnish my empty home for a photo shoot meant it could be included in this book. And Jenny Murphy: it makes me smile to see Lizzy being part of the furniture.

I owe special thanks to the sharpest pencil in Asia, Stephen McCarty ('"typology" – why not just "type"?') and to my early (and sometimes late) readers and editors: Thomas Schmidt, Matt Elkan, Kirsty Seymour-Ure, Suji Owen and Ron Rhodes (who also gave me my first newspaper job when I was still in pigtails). *M'goi sai* to a couple of photographers who lent me their editing and technical skills – May Tse and John Butlin, without whom my job as design editor at the *South China Morning Post* would be less tenable. Also to Ian Lambot of Watermark Publications, whose handsome architecture books have been an inspiration; Lucas Dietrich, Fleur Jones and Nick Jakins, of Thames & Hudson, for making my book a reality; and Matt Elkan again, for designing 2 + 2 House.

In sifting through my own photographs, I'm reminded of the many homes I visited that didn't make it into this book for space reasons or because I wanted to find different courtyard uses for each. Timing also played a part. I appreciate the help and enthusiasm of every architect I met for this project, and the stories they enabled me to tell.

Which brings me to my dearest, Max. This project could have taken half the time, but it would have been a fraction of the fun. That said, I am grateful you urged me to continue when there were practical reasons to stop collecting houses, as it were. Huge thanks also for exploring so many places with me after your work was done – and never once forgetting to take snaps! Without you, neither this book nor our courtyard house would exist.

INDEX

AUTHOR BIOGRAPHY

Charmaine Chan started her journalism career in Sydney and has since worked at newspapers and magazines in Tokyo and Hong Kong. She is Design Editor and Literary Editor at the *South China Morning Post* and an Advisor to the Hong Kong International Literary Festival. Charmaine has worked as Deputy Editor at the *Asia Literary Review* and as a writer focusing on architecture and design in Asia. A triple winner at the Newspaper Society of Hong Kong's Press Awards, she has a BA in Journalism from the University of Technology Sydney, and an MA in Japanese Studies from SOAS University of London. She can be found on Instagram @designunplugged

On the front cover: 17 Blair Road, Singapore, by Ong&Ong; photo credit: Aaron Pocock
On the back cover: Chameleon House, Indonesia, by Word of Mouth; photo credit: Daniel Koh Photography
On page 2: 2 + 2 House, Australia, by Matt Elkan Architect; photo credit: Desmond Chan, Lumos Imaging

First published in the United Kingdom in 2019 by Thames & Hudson Ltd, 181A High Holborn, London WC1V 7QX

This paperback edition published 2022

Courtyard Living: Contemporary Houses of the Asia-Pacific © 2019 and 2022 Thames & Hudson Ltd, London
Text © 2019 and 2022 Charmaine Chan
All images © 2019 and 2022 the copyright holders: see page 266

British Library Cataloguing-in-Publication Data
A catalogue record for this book is available from the British Library

ISBN 978-0-500-29679-0

Printed and bound in China by Toppan Leefung Printing Limited

Be the first to know about our new releases, exclusive content and author events by visiting
thamesandhudson.com
thamesandhudsonusa.com
thamesandhudson.com.au